LOGGING OUT

Your Guide to Redefining Success and Happiness in the Era of Social Media Dependence

By
LOONA EMBERS

© **Copyright 2023 - All rights reserved.**

The content contained within this book may not be reproduced, duplicated, or transmitted without direct written permission from the author or the publisher. Under no circumstances will any blame or legal responsibility be held against the publisher, or author, for any damages, reparation, or monetary loss due to the information contained within this book. Either directly or indirectly.

Legal Notice:

This book is copyright protected. This book is only for personal use. You cannot amend, distribute, sell, use, quote, or paraphrase any part of this book's content without the author's or publisher's consent.

Disclaimer Notice:

Please note the information contained within this document is for educational and entertainment purposes only. All effort has been executed to present accurate, up-to-date, and reliable, complete information. No warranties of any kind are declared or implied. Readers acknowledge that the author does not render legal, financial, medical, or professional advice. The content within this book has been derived from various sources. Please consult a licensed professional before attempting any techniques outlined in this book.

By reading this book, the reader agrees that under no circumstances is the author responsible for any direct or indirect losses incurred due to the use of the information contained within this document, including, but not limited to, — errors, omissions, or inaccuracies.

BluLight Homes & Digital Publishing
Regina, Saskatchewan, CA
thebookmaster@blulightpublications.com

TABLE OF CONTENTS

Introduction — 5

Chapter 1: The Rise of Social Media — 11
- History of Social Media — 11
- The Impact of Social Media on Our Lives — 26
- The Growing Dependence on Social Media — 35

Chapter 2: Social Media and the Quality of Personal Relationships — 39
- The Impact of Social Media on Communication — 39
- The Comparison Game: The Pressure to Present a Perfect Image on Social Media — 42
- The Importance of In-Person Interaction — 45

Chapter 3: The Pressure to Conform — 51
- The Role of Social Media in Shaping Our Self-Image — 51
- The Impact of Social Media on Our Mental Health — 54
- The Unrealistic Expectations Set by Social Media — 57

Chapter 4: Logging Out for Self-Reflection — 60
- The Power of Self-Reflection — 60
- The Benefits of Logging Out of Social Media — 65

Chapter 5: Tips on How to Avoid Excessive Social Media Exposure and Increase Focus — 72
- Understanding the Negative Effects of Excessive Social

Media	72
Setting Boundaries for Social Media Use	81
Finding Alternatives to Social Media	86

Chapter 6: Redefining Success — 91

Social Media's Impact on our Definition of Success and the Problem of Comparison	91
Tips on How to Set Realistic Goals and Value One's Definition of Success	96
Alternative Ways to Measure Success	100

Chapter 7: Finding Happiness Off-Screen — 107

The Importance of Finding Happiness Outside of Social Media	107
Ways to Cultivate Happiness Without Social Media	111
Strategies for Building and Maintaining Strong Relationships	113

Chapter 8: Building Real Relationships — 122

The Limitations of Virtual Relationships	122
The Importance of Building Face-to-Face Connections	125

Chapter 9: Building Resilience — 130

The Impact of Social Media on Our Resilience	130
Building Resilience in the Digital Age	135
Strategies for Overcoming the Negative Effects of Social Media	139

Conclusion — 149

INTRODUCTION

Imagine having a computer in your bedroom which allows you to talk to all your friends, family and colleagues. Or imagine being able to have access to all the information of the world right at your fingertips. What would happen if this power was switched on in a week, another ten weeks later, and again within another month? These phrases might sound like science fiction, but this is the reality we live in today. The rise of social media has completely changed how we go about our daily lives and how we relate with our fellow man. It has become an integral part of our lives, and no one can be considered independent anymore.

We all have experienced the same thing. Why is it so hard to resist the temptation of social media? Spending more time in front of our social media applications makes us less happy and less satisfied with our lives. Something seems wrong, but what can we do about it?

In this book, I will share tips to help you live a happier life without relying on social media.

A study by the University of Gothenburg, Sweden, published in February 2017, found that a third of the participants reported spending more time on their smartphones than with friends, family, or co-workers. The study also showed that people who used social media the most tended to be less happy than those who spent more time with real-life interactions. Another study conducted by researchers from Michigan State University has revealed that people who use social media extensively feel worse about themselves and have more anxiety. This is true even if they upload positive posts because they constantly compare themselves with others.

Two out of every three people suffering from chronic stress could be helped by eliminating or reducing social media use. The culprit is the negative comparison between one's own life and the "perfect" life presented by others on social media. This is especially prevalent on Instagram, which is used to showcase only the daily highlights of one's life and serves as a platform for seeking approval from other users through likes and comments.

Are you worried about the impact of social media on your mental health? Do you feel anxious when you look at your notifications only to find that no one has liked or commented on your posts? Have you ever felt like quitting social media cold turkey but don't know how to stick with it? If so, then this book is for you. It will introduce you to a new world called "real life." This book is divided into ten chapters. Each chapter will discuss various aspects of social media, how it affects our lives, and how we can start living more meaningful lives without it.

This book presents different strategies to overcome the negative impact of social media on happiness and mental health. We will explore how to use social media more effectively and choose the activities that will make a difference. By learning how to manage our time, we can spend it more productively and be happier. Optimizing our self-presentation and using social media for self-reflection will help us to understand our goals and stay inspired and motivated. The book is for people who want to live in the real world instead of a virtual one, for those who find it hard to resist social media's temptations, for those who feel anxious when they look at their notifications only to find that no one has liked or commented on their posts. The best part of this book is that by the time you finish reading it, you will be ready to begin your journey toward a happier life.

I have dealt with this topic in the past and have learned a lot from it. However, this is the first time I have shared my insights with people facing the same challenges as I did. I believe that you will enjoy this book and find it extremely helpful. This book was written not to make you a social media expert but to help you achieve what you always wanted, a happier life without depending on social media. Start spending less time on it and more time in real life to be happier. You can do this by controlling your time and managing your digital footprint more effectively.

After much research and study, I wrote this book to share my findings with others. The aim is to help readers identify their problems and should not be considered a complete resource for solving all their issues. It is more about awareness than about solving problems. You are probably right if you think this book will help you solve your problems. If not, that is okay too. After reading this book, I hope you will feel fulfillment and accomplishment because the day will come when you can enjoy life without being dependent on social media. In this book, I will share tips to help you be happier by getting off social media. I will explain the harm of overusing it and why it can affect your mental health if you don't set effective boundaries. I will also recommend some alternative ways to measure success in life without the need for social media.

This book will explore the beginning of social media and how it has changed our lives. While most people would agree that it has been a great innovation that has changed the way businesses communicate and how we stay in touch with our loved ones, few people understand how it changes our minds and affects our happiness. We will understand why we are so compelled to use social media and how it impacts us positively and negatively.

We will try to understand how social media has changed how we interact with friends and family. We will learn how it has made connecting with others more difficult and why it affects our relationships negatively.

As we proceed, we will focus on the impact of social media on our self-confidence and self-esteem and how it makes us feel depressed. We will understand why we are so desperate to be accepted by others, why social media pressures us to conform, and how it can give us an illusion of being connected to the outside world. But we are less connected to the outside world than we think. We will understand the illusory nature of Facebook and how it affects our self-reflective thinking.

Social media is great; in many ways, it has helped us build friendships and business relationships. Working on social media can be hard, especially for those people who find it difficult to stop using it. It is time to change our habits and learn how to live a happier life without the need for social media. This book will open your eyes and help you understand why taking action and changing your life is important. The time has come for us to let go of social media, spend quality time with our family and friends, and find happiness outside the screen. If you are ready to start, then there is no reason why you should delay.

CHAPTER 1

The Rise of Social Media

History of Social Media

Over the last decade, social media has become an essential part of many people's lives and an integral aspect of our culture today. Although it has helped to make the world smaller, it has also created many problems that were not there before. People's time on social media has increased dramatically over the last few years. It is such an important part of our lives nowadays that many people can't imagine a world without it. We are so attached to social media that we cannot even imagine not using it every day. Even when we are not using it, we are still thinking about it and dreaming about it, wasting more time and resources in the process. How did social media come to be, who is responsible for its current popularity, what is the harm of overusing it, and why has it become so difficult to disconnect from it? The next few chapters will try to answer these questions in a way that will enable you to understand how social media has affected your life.

However, before moving forward with this discussion, let's pause and take stock of where social media came from. It has become so widespread that you can't spend a day in modern society without hearing about it. But what exactly is it, and how did it come to be?

Social media is a relatively new phenomenon that has only gained popularity within the last decade. Still, its history can be traced back decades. Social media is an extension of the so-called "social revolution" in the 1950s. It was in the 1950s when people first started using it, primarily through the advent of television and telephone services. Television became a household item during this time, while phones made it possible for people to talk to each other over great distances. This also marked a new era where people could connect without seeing each other face to face. While the advent of television and telephone services helped people connect, it created new social problems. People now had to deal with various issues, such as privacy invasion and intrusive forms of communication. The use of television and phone calls in the 1950s marked the beginning of the modern telecommunication era when people invented many new ways to be connected.

The first social media platforms that followed were computer-based, such as bulletin board systems (BBS) and multi-user dungeons (MUD). These tools were quite popular in the 1980s. However, they eventually faded out due to their inability to overcome various computer-related issues. Therefore, it was not until the early days of the internet era that social media truly took off. In the early 1980s, many new networking and chat platforms were born. By the late 1980s, social media had become so popular that people started using it daily. As mentioned, many social networking sites and chat rooms during this era used the popular BBS and MUD systems. These platforms included features such as email, messaging boards, and instant messaging services, eventually leading to the birth of modern-day social media platforms that are so familiar today.

Social media platforms that were to become popular in the early 1990s were not necessarily seen as good at the time. Most of them did not even have names. These social media tools included Slashdot, Juno, and Cyberia. The development of these new internet tools was fueled by a need for entrepreneurs to satisfy their customers' needs for conveniently getting content or information from various sources.

Around this time, individuals offered most web content and networking services for free rather than being provided by companies or organizations. The first web-based commercial service was created in 1995 by Tripod.com, a free hosting service for people on the internet. Its name has now changed to Tripod.com, and it is still one of the most popular social media platforms today. Although there were many similar services then, they were not as successful as Tripod. They did not last long enough to compete with this popular social media site.

Another interesting fact about early web-based commercial services is that they didn't even have proper names. Instead of having names, they were generally referred to by their addresses or URLs, such as Yahoo! and Geocities. As the years passed and the internet became more accepted, many web-based commercial services like Tripod became social media platforms.

During this period, the term "social media" was not widely used and was referred to as "new media." In 1997, a group of Harvard graduates created one of the first social networking sites called SixDegrees.com. This site was less popular than Tripod, but it was still one of the most popular social media platforms during that time. However, Tripod still outpaced all other sites in popularity and reputation.

By the end of the 1990s, many people had already used social media to expand their social circle and friendships. These platforms also helped people find new friends, partners, and jobs. The site Friendster, launched in 2002, became one of the most popular social media sites. Over 3 million users adopted it within a few months. However, despite its popularity among users, it was not commercially successful for a long time because it did not have any business model to support this type of service. Therefore, in 2004 the site was sold to a company called MOL Global for $30 million.

In 2004, another popular social media site, Facebook, came into existence when some college students at Harvard created an unofficial online network known as "Facebook." It helps people create profile pages, build relationships, and share information. The site was initially only available to Harvard users; however, in 2005, it began to be accepted by other universities such as Yale, Michigan, and Cornell. Shortly after that, hundreds of other universities joined the network, and the number of Facebook users increased exponentially. As more colleges joined the network, other social media tools became popular among these groups.

Facebook was a social media tool that provided users with a more interactive and personal experience than many other sites at that time. This made it one of the most popular platforms in history as far as its user base is concerned. In 2006, MySpace was also launched, another popular social media platform. It was created as a social networking site for bands, musicians, and music lovers. Therefore, it was used by various professionals in the entertainment industry.

Unlike Facebook, MySpace accepted all applicants willing to join its community; however, it only became popular later. At the beginning of 2006, the number of users of MySpace was lower than 30 million; however, a mere year later, this number had already jumped to 100 million! During that time, MySpace had become one of the most popular social media platforms. It communicated with over 100 million people. Another popular social media platform at that time was Bebo. Bebo was initially created by one of MySpace co-founders and was another social networking site for people who were into entertainment. Bebo's popularity peaked in 2007 and became one of history's most visited social media platforms within just a few years.

During this era, "social media" described many similar websites and services that were not necessarily about sharing information or connecting with others for pleasure. The term "social media" was created by linking the terms "media" and "social" which described these platforms. Hence, social media's main objective was to enhance social interaction and help people easily share their thoughts with friends and family.

Soon social media platforms and services were not just used for fun; they became a part of people's daily lives. Many job recruiters started using these tools regularly. Companies began researching how to use social media to promote their goods or services. This is known as SMO or Social Media Optimization, the process by which people try to optimize their presence in one or more social networks to gain more traffic or consumer awareness.

Many companies began trying to make their brands more visible on these sites. For example, in 2011, a footwear company named Crocs, founded by one person named Wayne Chodoian, started using social media platforms to increase its brand visibility. After the company was sold to KKR for around $200 million, it started using social media platforms as a marketing tool to serve its customers and gain more market exposure. Unfortunately, the company soon discovered that this marketing campaign did not work well because many other companies were doing the same thing.

After Facebook became popular, several other social media platforms emerged. One of these was LinkedIn, created by Reid Hoffman, the COO of PayPal. This platform allowed people to create profiles to connect with others and start professional relationships. Moreover, LinkedIn also provided businesses with another outlet to promote their goods and services. It became the most popular social media platform for businesses.

Another popular platform that emerged during this era was Twitter, launched in 2006 by Jack Dorsey and Evan Williams, who had previously started Odeo which no longer operates. Twitter's main objective was to create a microblogging and social networking platform which meant its users could post short messages or updates rather than long blog articles. Twitter also included additional features such as direct messaging, news following, events, and email service. However, this website has not been as successful as other platforms because many people have misused it by posting spam and irrelevant information on their accounts.

One of the main reasons why these sites became so popular in such a short time is that they offered a completely different experience to many people who had previously used other similar websites. For example, people could easily share their thoughts with others entertainingly by posting messages on these sites. Moreover, sites like Facebook and Twitter allow people to share photographs and videos with their friends without problems because they do not have to upload them on other websites first.

In addition, social media platforms such as Facebook enable users to create groups based on their interests and hobbies. These groups enabled people to share pictures or content quickly and easily. Sites like Twitter also helped businesses connect with other businesses as well as customers in an easier manner. Many organizations also use Twitter to promote their products through tweets or retweets. Moreover, other sites, such as Instagram, emerged during this period. Instagram allows people to photograph their daily lives and share these images with their friends. Some of the pictures uploaded on Instagram were regularly used as "Say It With A Picture" memes by many people who enjoyed sharing these images with others.

Social media usage increased in 2012 when President Obama became the first United States president to join a social networking site. He created a Facebook page, which many fans and supporters used. He was also considered the first president with a successful social media marketing campaign. President Obama reached out to millions through this media during his time in office.

In the same year, Google+ also came into existence. This platform is another great example of how businesses can use social media to their advantage.

Google+, created by one ex-employee of YouTube and a co-creator of Google Play named Vic Gundotra, provided businesses with another prominent way to promote their goods or services to online users on other websites. Google+ was a great platform for businesses to promote their products and services.

Social media platforms such as Facebook and Twitter were not completely unregulated. They had rules concerning how users should use them. For example, Facebook stated that anyone using the platform must agree to its Terms of Use, meaning they agreed not to post anything offensive or inappropriate. However, many people in the 2010s still thought it was acceptable to post various types of material on these sites without monitoring it. In addition, Twitter also had rules that users had to agree to be able to use the platform. It was barred from advertising on its platform, and it was not allowed to show tweets or other direct messages that were publicly available.

Young people's social media usage became a common phenomenon in the 2010s. Many people, including teens and young adults, created their profiles on outlets like Facebook, Twitter, or Tumblr. They did this to share photos of their friends with one another and receive updates about their lives. Many young professionals use LinkedIn and Google+ to connect with colleagues and potential employers. Many young people considered social media an important part of their lives during the 2010s.

Social media was not the only site where people shared information with others. Some other sites emerged during this period, which many people used. For example, a Reddit site was launched in 2005 by Steve Huffman and Alexis Ohanian, who had previously created another online community called DIGG, which was closed in August 2010 due to various problems within its management team. However, Reddit is considered one of the most popular websites today because millions worldwide have used it. It is a news platform where people can submit links or photographs, watch videos, and even vote. The main aim of Reddit was to offer a forum-like area where people could share information about various topics which interested them. Individuals could create their own "sub" or section on Reddit to post any content relating to their favorite subject matter.

Reddit's usage grew rapidly during the 2010s because it offered something similar to other social media platforms but in its unique way.

Since this period, many other social media sites have emerged that are popular today, such as Instagram, YouTube, Pinterest, and Snapchat. Although Instagram was created in 2010, it was only launched in 2012. That was mainly because its engineers and designers needed time to create a better site than the one they had previously developed. However, with the small number of users of Instagram, this did not negatively affect its popularity worldwide because people continued to use Instagram's other features, such as "Stories" and "Lenses," regularly. YouTube was another site launched in 2005 but gained more popularity during the 2010s. This website was created by three former PayPal employees, Chad Hurley, Steve Chen, and Jawed Karim. The three men started YouTube to create a platform where users could share videos freely. They believed they had created a site that would change how people viewed content online.

There was also a Pinterest site, which Ben Silbermann, Paul Sciarra, and Evan Sharp created in 2010. Initially, this platform was used for sharing online content, such as photographs and images, before it became popular for sharing other types of material, such as news articles or messages. Pinterest also started growing during this period and became popular around 2013. This site is primarily known for being used as a way of sharing cool images with others. In 2014, it was stated that more women than men used Pinterest and that this trend was likely to continue.

Snapchat emerged during the 2010s and became one of the most popular social media sites today. Although it is mainly known for being used by people to send each other photos or videos which disappear within a few seconds, many other features were added to Snapchat as well, such as "Discover," "Live Stories," and a filter system called "Lenses." The filter system became popular on Snapchat because people could use facial blurring or other effects to look more interesting in their photographs or videos.

TikTok, a photo-sharing platform created by a Chinese woman named Anne Xie, also emerged during this period. According to reports, it had become the most popular social media application among young people in China by 2017 and currently has users from around the globe. This site primarily focuses on sending videos to other users rather than sharing photographs, as many other social media sites did during the 2010s.

People's usage of these websites has been growing since the beginning of their creation because they offer new and exciting ways for individuals to connect with their friends or other people interested in similar subjects.

Another big change concerning social media appeared in 2014: the emergence of "live streaming" sites such as Twitch and YouNow. Since this period, many people have been able to watch others play games or do other activities, allowing the user to show off their skills in front of their audience. Live streaming sites became so popular during the 2010s that they have overtaken social media sites as one of the most important ways for people to communicate with each other.

Overall, introducing social media platforms and services was a major boon for most people who used to spend hours on the internet. It offered them a different experience altogether. These sites made it extremely easy for people to communicate with others worldwide without any hassles. But they have been responsible for several security lapses and privacy concerns.

One of the major concerns about using these sites was that users had to provide certain information about themselves, such as their name, address, or email to create an account. Since this information was available publicly, anyone could view it. This led to numerous scams, hoaxes, and frauds that one could not easily differentiate from the original products.

One of the biggest concerns about using these sites was that some people posted malicious content about others or organizations. For example, in 2008, a 14-year-old girl named Megan Meier committed suicide after her friends created a fake profile on myspace.com. Several experts have cited this case as an example of how social media platforms could lead to psychological problems in users. Moreover, since these websites were always accessible, they became a perfect medium for stalkers or terrorists to create fake profiles and use them for illegal purposes.

This raises several ethical concerns about using social media platforms and the need for online privacy. For example, state of Sarawak in Malaysia uses social media networks to arrest offenders charged with certain crimes. Another issue related to online privacy concerns is that many companies try to find information about you from other internet sources and then post it on their websites or services for promotional purposes.

Several risks are also associated with using these sites. For example, some people may use these websites to make inappropriate comments or posts about others. These statements can be embarrassing for the person and can even lead to serious issues such as court cases. In addition, there are instances where fake profiles have been created to invade a person's privacy by harassing or stalking them. However, social media networks and platforms are still immensely popular; most people now use these sites regularly to connect with others worldwide. One must learn how to use these sites correctly to ensure that they don't get into serious physical or financial problems.

Social media has played a huge part in the development of the internet. These two platforms have been used by many people worldwide and are unlikely to die out at any point in the future. Their popularity will likely continue to grow because they provide services people want to use and need regularly. For example, social media sites allow users to share their thoughts with others, communicate with friends and family members from all around the world, and even keep up to date with what is happening in the news or various events that are taking place. In addition, these sites also allow users who cannot afford expensive mobile phones or other technology products an easy way to access the web instead.

The Impact of Social Media on Our Lives

The massive development of technology is changing the way our world operates. Many people spend significant time on social media, chatting or messaging loved ones or friends worldwide. However, we must ensure we are responsibly using these sites and not use them to annoy our family, friends, and others. Social media has had an incredible impact on our lives because it is used by many people worldwide to engage with each other without having to pay for anything. Social media allowed users to meet new people and friends in various countries. It has helped people to express their feelings, thoughts, and dreams with each other all over the world. This helps them become more cultured because it helps them learn about different places they have never heard about.

Impact on Business

Social media has also helped business owners grow their businesses because it is a good platform to reach many customers worldwide. Businesses can advertise their products and services on social media, making them more popular in the market. For example, Facebook has serviced millions of customers worldwide using Facebook adverts and other marketing strategies.

This also changes how businesses operate because they are forced to provide better customer service to attract new customers and increase earnings. The fact is that most people these days are willing to put up with mediocre customer service. Still, they will avoid companies that do not provide good customer service.

No one can ignore the impact of social media because the internet has serviced billions of customers worldwide, and this number will likely to increase over time. The truth is that most people now rely on social media for everything. They use social media to find information about what is happening daily and make new friends or relationships with people.

Social media has caused companies to grow because it allows them to communicate with their customers and clients, which ensures that they will continue using the products and services provided by these companies. Companies can spread the word about their products or services by advertising them on social media. For example, businesses such as Facebook can promote their products and services or even ask customers for feedback and opinions, which helps business owners to improve the quality of the products and services they offer.

Impact on Education

There has also been a significant impact on how we educate our students. This is because social media sites such as Facebook and Twitter allow teachers to provide their students with information and lessons and to document homework they may have.

Social media platforms have allowed millions worldwide to access information regarding different topics, including economics, politics, and science. All these topics are extremely important in our everyday lives. Social media allows us to learn about these things without spending money buying books or other expensive items.

Social media has allowed classroom students to express their feelings and thoughts to each other. Most teachers allow students to use sites like Facebook and Twitter when studying.

Social media has changed how education is carried out worldwide because it allows students to communicate with each other which helps them complete homework assignments and research various topics covered in class. Social media platforms have also helped students who live in rural areas learn about various topics, including geography and history because they can post questions or comments on these websites. Online collaboration between students is good because they can communicate anywhere. They can hold themselves accountable by looking at each other's work, content, and even videos or photos on the platforms they use daily. Students can also meet new people, make new connections, and even learn about different places worldwide. Social media is important for students because they can do these things daily.

Impact on Health

Social media has also had a significant impact on the health of people all over the world because people can use it to look for information about various diseases, symptoms, and even treatments for an issue they may have. People can ask questions and receive answers regarding health-related issues. For instance, they can ask a question regarding a certain disease and receive an answer from an expert in that field.

Social media has helped people who are sick to connect with others suffering from the same condition, allowing them to share their feelings, thoughts, and even stories about the condition they are suffering. Doctors and medical professionals can also post notes that they are using a certain medicine to treat a specific ailment. People can go online and read the notes posted by others who have suffered from the same condition. Online collaboration will never be replaced. Everyone worldwide must share and learn about different diseases, symptoms, and treatments.

Social media has helped people who suffer from diseases such as cancer or other terminal illnesses gain better knowledge about their illnesses while also helping them feel better about themselves. This is because people can talk about the problems that they are facing and how they can overcome them, making people who suffer from illness feel better about themselves. They can hear from other people who have gone through similar experiences. Social media has helped those suffering from illnesses, diseases, or terminal illnesses because they learn about their condition and how to overcome it.

Social media platforms allow users to post messages or stories regarding their disease and how they overcame it. For example, someone with cancer could post a message about how they beat the illness, encouraging others who suffer from the same condition.

There is a high chance that social media will continue to impact health and medicine because people can use it as an online research tool that they

can access anytime they want to learn about different diseases, illnesses, and treatments.

Impact on Entertainment

Social media has also significantly impacted the entertainment industry because it has allowed millions and millions of people to connect with others who share their interests. For example, you can go online and find out what movies, television shows, or music a specific person enjoys by going online and looking at the posts of that person. Social media allows you to view the people they follow, their friends, family members, and other people who have similar interests. This is extremely important because it allows users to learn about new artists or bands before hearing elsewhere. People can also find out what events are being held worldwide that they would like to attend. Social media has allowed people to make new friends and connections worldwide and make new contacts they would like to work with in the future.

Impact on Lifestyle

Social media has significantly impacted our society and other parts of the world because it allows us to connect in many ways. For example, we can interact with thousands of people online daily without being face-to-face. We can do so through social media platforms like Facebook, Twitter, and Pinterest. People can connect differently, depending on how they use social media. For example, using Instagram, you can interact with other people by looking at their photos and commenting. You can also post your photos and connect with those who like or comment on your posts. Social media can allow people to form new friendships, make new connections, and even meet strangers with similar interests.

People can connect with others in various ways online through social media because it allows users to share their thoughts, feelings, and even photos regarding what is going on in their lives. For example, you can take photos of the places that you have visited and share them with other users. This is a great way to show people worldwide what places you have been to. You can also tell stories about your travels so others can learn about them. You may also become friends with someone who goes through what you are going through You can learn about your new friend and their life experiences.

Impact on People's Knowledge of the World

Social media has impacted how people learn about different life aspects worldwide. For example, people can connect with users from various parts of the world to learn about different customs, traditions, and even languages spoken in other countries. You can go online and learn about new customs from other users who go through similar experiences or have traveled to the same places that you have traveled. This is beneficial because it allows people worldwide to connect and learn new things about each country or part of the world.

Negative Impacts of Social Media

There are several negative impacts of social media too. Users who do not know how to use it well can fall for online scams and phishing links, leading to identity theft. Social media has made it easier for cybercriminals to steal personal information such as passwords, credit card details, and bank account information. This is why you should be careful when using social media because there are a lot of cybercriminals lurking on the web looking for people who have not protected their personal information well or have given out too many details about themselves.

a) Cyberbullying

Cyberbullying is a form of bullying where people threaten, harass, or even make physical threats against other people in an online community. It happens most often on social media websites and instant messaging platforms such as **LINE**, Facebook and Twitter. Social media has allowed cybercriminals to bully others easily because users can upload threatening videos and photos or write messages on social media sites. This allows them to expose others without knowing who they are or the true identity behind the bullying messages they receive. Cyberbullying has been linked to multiple suicides worldwide, as many people cannot deal with continuous bullying from others online.

b) Theft of Personal and Financial Information

Theft of personal and financial information happens more often through social media. This is because people have given away their credit card details, bank account details, and even their passwords when they have gone to the bank to use their debit cards or entered their online banking details on social media websites. This can lead to identity theft because cybercriminals can use the information for fraud.

c) Cyberstalking

Cyberstalking is a form of harassment from other users through social media. This happens when people receive unwanted messages, calls, or even threats from other users. Cybercriminals can use these platforms to stalk others, and it is becoming more common every year. Cyberstalking can also lead to suicide if the person being stalked cannot handle the stress of receiving messages from strangers worldwide.

For all reasons above, we must make sure we avoid these forms of social media attacks by being aware of what is going on and trying to steer clear of anything that may be negative. Social media has brought about profound changes in the way that people communicate with one another. It has changed how people speak, express themselves, and share information. We can learn about places we have never heard about through social media platforms like Facebook and Twitter. There are many benefits to using these social media platforms, and they can cause a lot of good for us as a whole if they are used correctly. We must know the dangers associated with social media and other internet activities.

The Growing Dependence on Social Media

Social media addiction is a growing problem today. Many studies are being conducted to determine why so many people are addicted to their devices. In 2012, it was found in a study by Brigham Young University that "more than half of the participants used Facebook more than once a day, with 15% using the platform more than 40 times per day." This shows that social media platforms can become addictive for some people, and we must try to prevent this from happening to us.

Social media addiction can be bad for our health because it can make us less social. This could cause problems in our professional life and with our family when they want to spend time with us, but we are too distracted by social media. We must avoid this addiction by spending time away from these devices.

Being addicted to social media is not a good thing because it can cause many problems. It may cause problems at work and negative effects on our performance. It can also cause problems in our personal lives, especially if we start to neglect our friends, family members, and loved ones due to being addicted to these platforms. The growing dependence on social media is becoming more of a problem each day. People are abandoning traditional forms of communication for these online platforms, including email, text messages, phone calls, and letters.

Social media addiction can start from the first day you join these websites. It can begin in your early teens or even younger, depending on what website(s) you join first. You might check your social media pages every five minutes, no matter what you do. It is not good because it can lead to other problems. If you check your news feeds several times an hour, you may need to step back from using social media and seek professional advice from someone who can help you with these issues.

The dependence on social media has mainly been caused by the number of social interactions we have with our friends, family, and loved ones. We can have several friends worldwide whom we only interact with daily, which can cause us to feel alone sometimes, especially if we do not hear from them for a while. We must avoid this by limiting our time on social media and keeping in touch with our friends in other ways, such as letter writing, phone calls, and face-to-face conversations.

Social media addiction is a major problem that affects people around the globe; we mustn't allow ourselves to be affected by this. Many people are open to the idea that social media is starting to hurt their lives. We must take care of our time and try to spend it wisely. We should only use social media platforms for legitimate purposes and not use them for illegal activities, such as fraud, stalking, and harassment.

The dependence on social media can be easily cured by finding the right professional help. People can overcome their addiction, allowing them to concentrate on their personal lives and what is important to them. People must take care of their time because it can lead to many problems if they waste time daily through these activities. Social media can be helpful, but it can also cause a lot of harm, and these issues should be avoided at all costs.

CHAPTER 2

Social Media and the Quality of Personal Relationships

The Impact of Social Media on Communication

Communication has become an integral part of social media. We may find ourselves massaging our feelings on Facebook and Twitter because these sites provide a venue for communication that is not always realistic. We can view pictures of other people and express ourselves in an emotional manner. We can also send messages to each other in a way that does not always indicate what we truly mean or how well the recipient may receive the message.

This is one reason many people have committed suicide because of social media over the past few years. It often gives us a false sense that the world is how we see it, and our feelings are often portrayed as the truth. This type of messaging is also ineffective because it does not always allow for an in-depth conversation with our peers. We may experience this if we receive a message from someone who does not know what they are talking about or if they say something without thinking about it first.

Another issue with social media messaging platforms is that they can be used incorrectly and can lead to misunderstandings and hurt feelings. This can happen when we do not read what another person says carefully enough or do not understand the message that the other person may be trying to send us.

Social media messaging can also be used to make jokes, leading to hurt feelings because these messages can be misunderstood and may not be true.

Social networking sites allow us to defend ourselves when we cannot do so in real life. This is because we have time to respond to a message, allowing us to craft what we want to say. It can be good because it allows us to avoid misunderstandings with our peers and can give us time to consider what we should say or how we should say it.

The problem with social media messaging is that there is no personal interaction. We cannot get to know each other in depth. This can lead to misunderstandings and hurt feelings, which can cause us to become angry or upset. This anger can be directed toward the people who sent us the message or toward ourselves.

The quality of friendships has been negatively affected by social media messaging. Many people feel a lack of connection with others because they tend not to know each other well enough on these platforms and cannot get to know these people deep down inside.

Many people have been led to believe that their connections through these sites are more than mere social connections. These friends we are close with on Facebook or Twitter have made us feel like we are stronger people, which is quite dangerous.

These sites have allowed us to connect with people worldwide and give us a sense of belonging. We can make friends from cultures that we would not normally be able to make friends with, allowing us to learn about other cultures and the world we live in.

Social media can hurt the quality of our relationships because it does not allow for face-to-face interaction. We may not always be able to tell what another person is feeling and thinking when we communicate with them online, which leaves room for misunderstandings and hurt feelings.

Social media has affected the quality of personal relationships in some positive ways because it allows us to communicate with others from different countries and cultures, allowing us to learn about these cultures, which can open our eyes to new things. We can also make friends online whom we would not normally meet in real life. This is an excellent thing for us emotionally because we feel accepted by these people who live all over the world.

Social networks allow us to become more connected with others around us, but this can only happen when we are open with each other. If we are not open with our peers, then these sites will not have the same impact on us as they otherwise would.

The Comparison Game: The Pressure to Present a Perfect Image on Social Media

Social media is an illusion because it gives the impression that people are happier and enjoying more success than we are. There is a lot of pressure to live up to what we see online because someone else may appear to have a perfect life, and they could seem perfect in every way. Social network sites give people the power to curate their lives, allowing them to decide which pictures they want to post on their pages, which videos they want others to see, and what information from their past they want the public to know about.

The first issue of comparing ourselves to others on social media is that it can create feelings of inadequacy. We may not always feel good about ourselves because we compare our lives to those we follow on social media. These sites provide a platform for comparing ourselves to those we follow because they put our lives on display. We can see what these people are doing, which gives us a sense of what others have that we do not have. This can lead us to feel like our lives have less value than the lives of others, making us feel inadequate in many ways.

Social networking sites allow us to present an image of ourselves that is quite different from who we really are. We can showcase our success on these sites and choose who will see what we share. This allows us to project the image that we want others to see, and it allows us to feel better about ourselves. However, this could lead us to think that our lives are better than they are because we have not given others a true account of who we are or what we do.

Social networking sites have allowed people to present an image of themselves as perfect, which gives others an unrealistic view of who they are and what they have accomplished in their lives. We may look at their images and feel like our lives do not measure up to the ideal life that they portray, leading people to not feel good about themselves. They can spend a lot of time stressing over the way they look, how they present themselves in public, and what others think of them. It can dilute our ability to be open and vulnerable with our peers.

We must know ourselves inside and out because this will allow us to feel happier with ourselves while cultivating confidence among those around us. This confidence will prevent us from becoming jealous of what other people have or who they follow on these platforms. Social networks have influenced how people feel about themselves and have made people more aware of the lives of others. This has caused people to compare their lives to those they follow online, leading them to feel inadequate in many ways.

We should be honest about our lives because this is an important building block for healthy self-esteem. We should seek out friends who tell us the truth because this helps us develop into happy and healthy adults.

Social networking sites have also influenced the way that people perceive themselves. People have become more aware of the lives of others, and this can make them feel like they are not living up to society's expectations. They may feel like what they are doing is not good enough and choose to hide behind the images they present on these sites. People who feel inadequate in this way can spend much time worrying about their appearance because they do not want to be seen as people others don't care about. If a person does care about them, it could make them jealous of other people's lives or accomplishments.

Social media has influenced how people feel about themselves because it has given them a platform to compare their lives to the lives of others. This could make a person feel like they are living in someone else's shadow and prevent them from feeling good about their life. Social networking sites impact our self-esteem because we can compare ourselves to others, which can cause us to feel inadequate in many ways. The comparison game is not a healthy or productive activity because it causes people to feel inadequate in many ways and can make them envious of other people's lives. We should all seek out friends who will understand us the way we are and help us improve in life.

The Importance of In-Person Interaction

In-person interaction refers to the time we spend with others in physical proximity, allowing us to communicate and interact with people because we can see and hear them as we talk to them. This is a different experience from interacting online because there is no way to gauge how others truly feel.

Through social media, users can connect with others from a distance, which has changed their relationships in many ways. For example, people can be more involved in other lives, leading them to neglect their own lives. We can't know how someone else feels about us when they communicate online or on the phone. They may lie to us because they are not interested in being honest, which can make us feel unsure of our relationships and cause us to be more involved in other people's lives than we want.

We need in-person communication because it allows us to see how others feel and what they may think about our lives. It gets into the real world so that we can see the true feelings of others when we interact with them. When we communicate with those in our lives, we can connect with them and know they are fundamental to us. This is what helps us see their true personalities and the way that they feel about themselves. Knowing how to act face-to-face may be challenging when people have complex online relationships. They may fear rejection or conflict. These things can ultimately lead to a breakdown of communication and relationships.

Social media has changed people's relationships because we can connect with others from a distance. We are no longer limited to the people physically around us because we can make friends worldwide.

When we interact with someone online or on the phone, it may feel like we know them, and this could cause us to have real feelings for them, which might not be the case when you meet them in person. This is complex because you could begin to care about people online after getting to know them for some time. Then when you meet them in person, it can be difficult to know how you truly feel about them. It will depend on who they are and how they present themselves.

Social media use can give people a false sense of connection with others because we can interact with someone at any time, which could lead us to think that we have known them forever. In reality, we may have just met the person or talked with them briefly on social media. It can be easy to spend a lot of time communicating with a person online because we can see how they live their lives from the outside looking in. As a result, these people may be more real to us than those physically around us. There is also no way to gauge how others truly feel about us when talking with them on social media.

Social media sites such as Whatsapp, Facebook, and Instagram have made it easier for people to maintain relationships. Our conversations can make them think they know each other better than those they have known in person. This is ultimately a false sense of reality because the people online may not be the same in person. When we can see what other people are doing online, it can cause us to care about them more. This can lead to a sense of loneliness that you did not know what you were missing and could make it harder for you to foster real relationships with those around you.

Catfishing is when people use fake pictures to create a false impression about someone. There have been various methods, and many people have tried to discover the best. It can be a complex thing to do because it is one of the risks you take when engaging in these types of activities. It is quite easy for people to use their social media accounts and real identities to create a false impression because they do not want anyone else to discover that they are doing something like this. This is the type of activity that people will try on social media sites with others they want to know more about. When you interact with another person face to face, you tend to avoid such things because it can be illegal to do something like this. If someone finds out you have done this with them, it can cause significant problems for your relationship.

Social media allows people to be whomever they want, which could ultimately lead them to make decisions they would not otherwise make. It is essential for people to interact with others in person because it is the only way that you will know what type of person they really are. Social media has created an alternative experience for people and has changed how many view themselves and their relationships with one another. When we are social with other people in person, it allows us to open up more to them. We can share feelings and emotions that we would not usually express online. We can break down barriers between ourselves and others because we do not see each other as mere "followers" but as real people with real feelings.

Social networking sites have made us more introverted and have caused us to care a lot about what others think about us. We are afraid of being judged for the things we share on these sites because our peers could see our faults or imperfections, leading them to perceive us differently from who we are. Social media allows us to create false personas because we can present ourselves in a way that will be seen in a positive light, which can lead people to believe that they know us better than they do, and this creates an alternative reality for our relationships with others. We can share things about ourselves from the past and present, allowing us to hide things we do not want others to see or know about.

Social media has made it easier for people to deceive each other because people are always connected, allowing them to show their true selves online. As a result, people can be a lot more open about their past and present relationships because they can learn about each other's backgrounds, giving them the impression that they know everything about each other. Social media will also make it easier for people to engage in cyberbullying because they can share things others should not see.

CHAPTER 3

The Pressure to Conform

The Role of Social Media in Shaping Our Self-Image

Social media is a potent tool that could influence how people see themselves. When we are connected to social media sites, it can influence the way that we share things about ourselves. We may share more positive things about ourselves because if we do not, our followers could think badly of us or even stop following us. One of the reasons why people use social media sites is to present themselves in a good light because people can judge them for the things they share online.

Social media has made it easier for people to conform to peer pressure, leading them to change their behaviors to fit in with like-minded others. When we are connected to social media, it can make us think that it is okay to do things that we may not otherwise do when we are not connected to these sites.

Social media has also made it easier for people to be less assertive because they will show things about themselves in a way that is different from the people around them. Social media has changed the way people can express themselves. It has allowed people to show the world their flaws and imperfections, and they could learn what others think of them because they will see their remarks on the internet.

The role of social media in shaping our self-image is vast because it changes how we view others and ourselves. It does not matter how you view other people and how you can see them for who they are.

Regarding shaping our self-images, social media could cause us to have distorted views of what we are like. It may be difficult for people to compare themselves because they do not see who they are personally. They may think they fit in with a particular group of people on social media, even though these groups may not exist in real life. People could lose confidence in their identity, becoming more introverted and socializing less with others. Therefore, people must realize how social media has changed how we interact with others and how it has shaped our self-images.

Social media can influence how we view ourselves because people may share things about themselves without being aware of what they are doing. People may look at pictures they post online, which could make them take much more pride in their identity. It could also make them question who they are as individuals because they may begin to understand the person they want to be.

When it comes to the view of ourselves, social media can make us feel self-conscious. We may feel we belong to a particular group of people on these sites, which could make us want to change who we are. We could think that we do not fit in with these groups, which could cause us to think about who we are. People can get ideas from celebrities or how they present themselves on social media sites because this can influence them to try new things.

We may change who we are when we look at what others present online, which could make us uncomfortable with who we are as individuals. People are not aware of the things that they share online, and this could cause them to feel uncomfortable with who they are. It is, therefore, important for people to ease their fears because they may be unable to control how they present themselves.

Social media allows people to present themselves in any way they want because there are no restrictions on using these sites. It can allow people to explore whom they want to be and influence them to try new things or change who they are. People should know what it means when someone says something about them on social media, which could make them self-conscious about who they are.

The Impact of Social Media on Our Mental Health

Since so many people use social media daily, most people have become connected to these sites, which has led to an increase in the amount of time people spend on them, which can be linked to mental health. There is an increase in the number of diseases that individuals can develop because they spend too much time looking at pictures and videos while they are connected to these sites.

There are several reasons why social media could be linked to mental health issues. It causes anxiety, depression, and isolation in people because we may see ourselves or other people behaving in specific ways through photos, videos, or articles written on the internet. It can cause us to feel inadequate because we may question the person we are and compare ourselves with others. It can also make us feel isolated because we may see so many negative things around us, which could cause our mental health to decline.

Social media has made it easy for us to be judgmental about ourselves because we may compare our lives with the lives of others on these sites. We could compare our bodies with other people's bodies because we see their pictures online. Social media has also made it easy for people to get hurt because they may see photos of the people they love in pictures with someone else.

Social media could contribute to sadness because we may see many negative things around us. This could cause us to think about what is happening and how these things affect us. It could also cause us to think about who we are as individuals because we may compare our lives with those of others on these sites. Mental health experts claim that this is more than just a problem for some – it has escalated to an epidemic slowly destroying the mental stability of millions of teenagers who are entering adulthood. Our obsession with social media grows daily, so we must start facing the truth about our loved ones being exposed to mental health problems. According to experts, this is especially dangerous for teenagers who are not yet mentally stable and do not possess the essential skills to process their thoughts and emotions.

Social media can have a little bit of a positive effect on mental health because it allows us to spend time with the people we love. It also allows us to share our honest thoughts, feelings, and experiences online, which can help us be more genuine and connect better with the people that we value the most. It is supposed to be a good thing, but it can also cause us to develop different mental health issues. It could even lead us to lose confidence in who we are, and this could cause us to become more introverted or socialize less with the people around us.

Social media has become a big part of our lives, but we are still unsure how it can affect our mental health. We may think we are becoming obsessed with these sites because there is so much pressure on people today to post things online and engage in social activities. We should take control over our actions on these sites; this will allow us to control how they affect our mental health.

Looking at social media sites can influence our physical health as well. There are links between having poor mental health and being overweight or obese because when you spend a lot of time looking at images on these websites, it starts to give you the impression that this is what you should look like.

There is pressure on people to look a certain way, and the use of social media sites could influence this.

People may see pictures or videos of t they admire, which could lead them to feel they need to be like them. Social media sites are doing more harm than good to our health, and we should start thinking about how we use these sites. The next time you check your phone or computer screen, try not to obsess over what is posted online.

The Unrealistic Expectations Set by Social Media

The use of social media creates unrealistic expectations because most people we see online are not real. They are actors, models, and other celebrities who pose in a certain way that they think looks good in captioned photographs or videos. We watch their lives and assume this is how our lives should look. A particular image of a social setting on social media is made for entertainment purposes only because these sites are not meant for us to base our life's decisions on what we see there.

This could cause us to feel depressed about ourselves and our lives because the unrealistic expectations set by social media sites can cause more harm than good to those using them.

The need to be "good enough."

Many people on social media sites feel the need to be noticed. They want to be popular because they think this will make them happy. They want their friends and family members to like them, and they are desperate for the attention of others. We see this in how our peers and friends use social media for entertainment. They post pictures of themselves to get the attention of others because they feel that this makes them better than their peers.

Most people on social media sites are attractive, which could pressure us to look a certain way because it makes us feel like we need to be attractive too. We can start comparing ourselves with others because we must be like them to fit into society. We may see pictures or videos of more attractive people, which could make us feel horrible about ourselves.

A lot of people who are using social media sites see them as entertainment. They spend time on these sites because they need to be entertained, and their brains get used to the constant action and excitement. The more you use these sites, the more you will want to be on them, and this will cause you to become addicted to them, and you will find it hard to stop using them.

We can change our lives by not spending as much time on social media sites as we do now. We are rarely alone when we log onto these sites, but if we were, we might realize that all these images are meaningless and that we are wasting our time by looking at them constantly. The next time you waste your time on social media sites, remember that these images and videos are not authentic, and you should focus on your life in the real world.

CHAPTER 4

Logging Out for Self-Reflection

The Power of Self-Reflection

Self-reflection is a powerful tool that can be used to help us identify our strengths and weaknesses. It will also allow us to take a step back, look at what's happening in our lives, and assess whether we are on the right path. Self-reflection is one of the most important things that needs to happen in the 21st century because it gives us a chance to look at things from a different perspective, one that we are not used to seeing because we are so caught up in living our everyday lives. It allows us to look at the big picture and re-evaluate our lives.

Self-reflection is a practice that has been around for decades. Still, due to the popularity of social media and other digital devices, it seems this activity isn't happening as much anymore. I feel that this is one of the reasons why humans aren't as connected with others anymore: they don't spend enough time alone (or looking at themselves) to reflect on their lives. People need to remember that self-reflection isn't supposed to be used to validate their happiness, but rather it is supposed to be used as a tool that will help them identify and change what isn't working in their lives. I think there will be times when you will feel overwhelmed by the amount of self-reflection that you need to do, and it can even make you feel like you're going crazy at times. It is expected because we are supposed to feel this way when we look at our lives.

Self-reflection should not be seen as a chore or something that happens occasionally. Instead, it should be seen as a way of living our lives. You don't do it for a few days and then go back to your old routines. It's something that you have to do daily. It helps us see things differently and what would happen if we changed some of the decisions we've made in our lives.

Self-reflection should be done as often as possible to constantly remind ourselves about where we are in life and whether or not we are on the right course. It's not about being happy always, but it should be about living the happiest life you can.

Commit to this daily to lose weight and get in shape. It would help if you created new habits to help you become fit and healthy. I'm not saying that you should spend your days in the gym but rather try different things that will allow your body to become more active throughout the day.

I used social media to disconnect myself from the online world to improve my self-reflection skills. Although social media is not the best way to do this, I was able to use it to help me look at myself in a way that I've never done before. It was easier for me because of the many stats that were available online, which meant that I could easily find out why certain things were happening and be able to explain them.

I realized that all of my interactions on social media were based around the following things – listening to other people's conversations and feelings, posting about how wonderful my life is or how great everyone else is, asking people what they think, or asking others if they want to talk about some things. If everyone responds with 'no,' it's not worth posting anymore. This is why social media has become such a problem for many people. It's all about what other people are doing, talking about, or feeling; things like this will never make you happy. It will always remove your focus from what you need to focus on. I think it's good to be aware of things like this because it helps us change our habits and improve our lives.

I understand that some people enjoy social media, so I don't have any problem with that, but I feel that excessive use of social media can cause real-world issues if people don't look at the bigger picture when using it. Being alone in a room and looking at yourself will help you to see what's happening in your life. Still, if you don't take the next step and spend some more time with others, you might not get to the fundamental truths hidden behind the negative feelings we get from social media.

Many fear being alone because they think it will weaken them or make them become someone else. I think this is because they were never taught how to be alone, so everyone needs to learn how to be alone (even though it might take some practice). We should do this before we can begin practicing any other social skill. Social skills should be learned and practiced long before we attempt to use them in the real world. It will help us learn important social skills and ensure we don't waste time practicing things that won't ever be used.

Remember that self-reflection is not about looking at your problems when you're unhappy with life but looking at what you have done right and learning from these things before you get stuck in a cycle of negativity.

When you are reflecting on your life, try to ask yourself these questions:

- What are the things that I enjoy doing in my life?
- What do I want to do but don't have the time?
- What do I think about when I look at myself in the mirror?
- Am I living a life that prevents me from being happy?
- When was the last time that I felt truly happy?

Doing this will help you identify what is happening in your life and whether or not you are on the right course. It will also show you where you stand when it comes to self-analysis. I reflected on my life the other day and decided to look at things I used to enjoy doing but don't anymore. This is something that has happened in the past, but it's something that should not happen in life. It helped me realize that if these things were removed from my life, it would be easier for me to start living a happier one.

My mind became active when looking at everything that was no longer available. Being alone and thinking about everything helped me realize how many things were missing from my life. I could see how many things I used to enjoy doing and how happy those activities made me feel in the past. I want to be clear, and this is not a negative thing. It's just that things you used to love or think were important are no longer a part of your life. Being alone and thinking about these things makes you see what has been lost and what remains in your life.

This exercise helped me realize what I needed to do because I could see everything missing from my life. This made me realize that I had a lot of work to do, so I needed to reflect on my life. When you are alone in your room or without distractions, take the time to think about what is important in life. It is one of the most important things to focus on when reflecting on your life. Doing this will help you focus more than anything else and allow you to use this time in a way that works for you.

The Benefits of Logging Out of Social Media

We live in a social world because we want to be seen and heard as much as possible. We want everyone to know what we are doing, feeling, and thinking at all times. Social media has given us a platform to make this possible and allows us to connect with many people worldwide. It allows us to communicate with them instantly via our computers or phones. No matter where we are in the world (or where they are), we can always communicate instantly and quickly through social media. It is something that many people love about it, but some forget that it can also harm us because we are not always in control of our actions. We cannot fully control everything that happens to us; because of this, we need to focus on the important goals in life.

One thing that I make sure to do every day is to keep myself away from social media sites as much as possible. I do this to make sure that I keep my mind active and focused on the important things in life. When you log off social media, it is much easier to regain focus and think about what you want to accomplish.

When we use social media, we become addicted to being connected with others, making it difficult to be alone (even though we are alone while using it). It's challenging to eliminate this negative habit, but breaking it is essential. You can disconnect from social media by walking through the park or anywhere with trees and plants.

By connecting with nature regularly, you can reconnect with your true self and think about the things that matter to you. You need to feel the oxygen coming out of the trees and plants around you, feel how nature works and how beautiful it is. This will help you become more aware of what is happening in life currently without being distracted. We will see what's happening around us when we become more aware. When we step away from our computers and mobile phones, it becomes easier to reflect on our lives and put our focus back on what is important in life. It allows us to consider the things that are missing from our lives.

We must remember because we tend to focus on things that make us unhappy. Whenever we are online, we are exposed to much bad and negative news about our lives. We are also exposed to other people's sadness and anger, making us feel bad. When you disconnect from social media, you can focus on making yourself happy again. I know this is easier said than done, but it's possible. Give it time, as it will help you begin thinking about what you want in life and working towards these goals. Too many people are not living the lives they deserve because they are stuck in the past or the present. They are not thinking about the future and what to do with their lives.

We must understand that we cannot change anything about our past (you cannot rewind time). But you can control your feelings about your past by changing your thoughts. It is also important to understand that focusing on being present will prevent us from thinking about our problems. We have so many problems in life, but when we focus on what is happening right here, all those problems will disappear, and life will become much easier.

When we log out of social media, there is less exposure to negative things. We can't always control what people say about us online, but we can control how we allow them to affect our lives. Whenever I'm on social media sites, I try and make the most of it by staying active with my friends and family. Then when I'm on my computer, I usually stay inactive for a long time. It helps me regain focus on the important things in life. We need to remember that it is still good in this world, and when you remove yourself from social media, all of the bad things will be less visible in your life and you will feel better. It's important to make sure that you understand this and will be able to apply it in your daily life. We often forget this because we get so used to being connected with others that we forget what it is like to be completely away from them.

When you are on social media, filter what people say about you, so you don't become distracted by anything negative or upsetting. This isn't easy at first because we become attached to how others view us. The best way to do this is by imagining that we are not reading any comments or messages from the people we relate to online. We can do this by pretending that we are talking to them in real life and telling them what we think about what they have said to us. This will help you understand that you have complete freedom over your thoughts and feelings and how others make you feel. When we are disconnected from social media, it is always important for us to take note of the positive things in life. I do this by imagining I'm on a beach during sunset with a beautiful sky (pink sky) and a beautiful background without any buildings or tall trees around me.

Another benefit of logging out of social media is that you will realize how much easier it is to free your mind and think about important things. You will also begin feeling relaxed and calm because you are no longer exposed to all the bad news out there. Social media can cause us stress and anxiety because we tend to focus on the bad things. I know that it's not easy to eliminate social media from our lives, but it is possible if we give it time. It's also important for us to remember that if our social media activity makes us feel unhappy or depressed, then we need to make a change for the better. We can do many things with our lives to give us a higher sense of fulfillment.

Most smartphones have a detailed usage screen showing your time on social media. It is found in the settings menu and measures the time spent on each social media network. This great tool will allow us to understand how much time we spend on these sites. Using this as a reminder is also important because it will allow us to track our progress over time. This is a good way to understand how much time you spend online. If we want to change, we must analyze our activity honestly.

If you want to improve your life, you should consider logging off social media and doing something meaningful with your life. You can learn how to meditate or go for a long walk through the park. You can also read a good book or get involved in a movement that focuses on empowering and helping others. We have many options, but most people will not take advantage of them. They are too busy staying home and doing the same things. They will feel like they are living in prison without real purpose. I know it's not easy to escape this prison, but giving it time and dedicating yourself to positive change is possible.

Social media can be addicting; whenever we leave something we are addicted to, we tend to miss its associated experiences (good and bad). People develop disorders and diseases because of their addiction to certain substances, such as alcohol and drugs. We can have an addiction to social media just like these people have a problem with alcohol and drugs. So, if this sounds like you, then try and remove yourself from social media for a while so that you can learn how to live without it. Don't hate on others addicted to it but try your best to do the same if you want life to improve. We must understand that we only focus on what is wrong in life and not see things that were once wonderful.

If we disconnect from social media, we will discover how beautiful our lives are.

CHAPTER 5

Tips on How to Avoid Excessive Social Media Exposure and Increase Focus

Understanding the Negative Effects of Excessive Social Media

Many people complain about their life and how fake and unsatisfying it is. They do this because they have problems with overindulgence in social media and the amount of exposure involved. This excessive use of it can cause stress because we always compare ourselves to others when considering ourselves more successful or popular. Most people fail to realize that there is no right or wrong path in life, but what matters the most is that we develop a positive approach based on our experiences and actions.

Getting caught up in a whirlwind of bad experiences when you spend too much time on social media is easy. Many teenagers have no real friends and cannot get into a job because they haven't learned how to communicate with others that aren't on social media. We need to learn how to communicate with others and make ourselves more interesting without being exposed to social media all day.

Let's take a look at the negative effects of excessive exposure to social media.

Social Media causes us to have Poor Communication Skills.

Social media causes us to become more self-centered because we constantly post pictures and updates of ourselves online. As a result, this makes it harder for us to communicate with others, as we aren't hearing what they're trying to tell us anymore. Because of how much time we spend making and posting these updates about ourselves all day long, this can cause our communication skills to suffer.

Social Media Engages us in Competitive Thinking and Sensitive Behavior

When we spend too much time on social media, we think about the good things others say about us. However, we also think about bad things. This thinking happens because we spend much time comparing ourselves to others. Their actions also upset us because they are rude and aggressive toward us.

Social Media Linked to Poor Decision-Making Skills

When you spend a lot of time online, you get completely distracted from what you need to do. You begin focusing on the wrong things that others post about you, making it difficult to think about anything else. As a result, it is easy for you to make bad decisions because your attention is focused on negative information rather than all the good things happening around you.

Social Media can Lead to Depression and Social Anxiety

If you have a problem with depression, social media will only worsen your situation. We need to limit our exposure to social media because it allows us to develop feelings of inadequacy, eventually leading to depression. When we feel depressed, we lose control over our lives because we begin seeing the world in a way that makes us pessimistic about everything. We also become more anxious when we leave things like Facebook and Twitter open all day because it allows others to see what we are doing.

Social Media Can Increase Our Levels of Stress

One of the most common negative effects that social media causes is increased stress. It happens because we start comparing ourselves to others and feel insecure about our lives. We must understand that the things we see on social media will never be as good as those others post. We then start seeing the world in a more stressful manner because we worry about other people and what they say about us.

Social Media Can Cause Breakdowns from Overthinking

You often spend too much time thinking about what other people have posted online, which leads to overthinking. On top of this, you become extremely paranoid because you keep thinking that people are reading your thoughts and know everything about you. We need to understand that social media is a huge distraction that we want to find ways to limit.

Social Media Causes Us to Lose Connection with Our Friends

Social media can cause us to lose connection with our friends and family because it alienates us from the material world. We spend too much time online, which causes us to neglect our real lives and problems. As a result, we start losing interest in our friendships and focus on what others have posted about them online instead of who they are.

Social Media Causes Us to Lose Interest in the World Around Us

If we spend too much time on social media, we lose interest in everything around us. We only see the negative things other people post online and start focusing on our lives instead of what is happening around us. This can lead to people becoming completely isolated from the world and forgetting how amazing it is. As a result, you will stop participating in all the events around you because you aren't interested in them. After all, they aren't about you.

Social Media Causes Negative Interaction with Others

Because we spend too much time looking at other people's profiles and reading the bad things they have posted, we get more negative towards ourselves and others. As a result, we become extremely depressed and withdrawn because we feel like everyone else is more interesting than we are, which causes us to become jealous of the people who have succeeded without having an online presence. We also lose interest in interacting with others because we don't trust them or feel they are better than us somehow.

Social Media Causes Us to Have an Unrealistic Perception of Success

Since we spend a lot of time on social media, this gives us an unrealistic perception of success because we only see people with Facebook pages who post good things about themselves. After all, they mostly post the things they buy and their pictures, even though many are unsuccessful. As a result, we think everyone else is better off than we are when they aren't. So, we must understand that social media can hinder our success if we leave it open all day.

Social Media Causes Us to Act in a Passive-Aggressive Way

Because we spend too much time looking at everyone else's profile updates instead of interacting with the people around us, this causes us to act passive-aggressively. We begin to get mad at the people who have posted things about themselves that make them look good or feel jealous of the things they have in life. We also get angry because other people post about them instead of us. This can make us frustrated and develop a negative outlook on everything.

Social Media Can Lead to Sexting

Because we spend too much time looking at pictures on social media, it is easier for children to develop an interest in sexting. As a result, they spend more time sending photos back and forth with other minors that are their friends or acquaintances. As a result, they may send naked photographs of themselves to others after doing so with their friends and family members, which can make it harder for them to tell the difference between reality and fantasy because they aren't sure how things are in the real world anymore.

Social Media Causes Us to Become More Jealous of Others

One of the biggest negative effects of social media on our lives is that it causes us to become more jealous of others around us. As a result, we start focusing on what others want and feeling bad about ourselves because we feel left out. We also start doubting ourselves and think we have less value than others due to what we see people posting about them online, making us feel insecure about ourselves and focusing on our appearance and what we do all day.

Social Media Causes Us to Lose Interest in Risky Behaviors That Can Lead to Addiction

Because we spend too much time looking at what other people post about themselves online, this causes us to lose interest in risky behaviors that can lead to addiction. It is because we see that they have posted pictures or social media updates where they are taking drugs or doing other dangerous things. As a result, we think it's not worth the risk and decide not to participate in these activities anymore. We also think it's cool when others do these things but don't want to participate because of the dangers.

Social Media Causes Us to Become More Socially Anxious

Because we spend too much time looking at other people's pictures and social media updates, this causes us to become more socially anxious. As a result, we begin to worry about what people think about us. We try to control how we look online because it could be why someone dislikes us. But because of how many online social media accounts there are, this can make it harder for us to control how we look and post.

Social Media Can Lead to Decreased Self-worth

Spending too much time on social media makes us start thinking about other people's lives more than our own and what they want instead of what we want, which can cause us to act as if we are not important and are just there for someone else's amusement. As a result, we start focusing on other people's needs and not our own. This makes us feel like we aren't being taken care of and aren't important to anyone anymore, and it causes us to feel depressed about it.

Social Media Causes Us to Act in an Unhealthy Way

Because many people spend too much time on social media, this causes them to act unhealthily. Research has shown that being addicted to social media is linked with depression and anxiety disorders among adults. It's also been proven that this addiction may be responsible for a rise in the competitive eating disorder since people post pictures of their meals all the time, which can cause us to become obsessed with how we look and eat.

Social Media Causes Us to Be Self-Conscious

Because so many people spend too much time on social media and compare themselves to everyone else, this causes them to become more self-conscious about how they look and act. As a result, they begin taking more time preparing to go out or meet new people because they feel like they need to look good online. This can also cause us to spend more time preparing for events than enjoying them.

Social Media Causes Us to Become More Impulsive

Because we spend too much time looking at social media we can become more impulsive in our daily lives because we see what other people are doing online, which causes us to want to be part of those things more than anything else in life. Because of how many images there are on social media, this makes it easier for us to become influenced by other people's opinions. We could easily think they know best and start following their lead instead of our intuition or common sense.

These and many more are the negative effects of social media that have been discovered and reported. Having a good balance between social media and life is not easy because we are so used to spending a lot of time on it. When you are connected with others all the time, you become addicted and lose most of your focus in reality, which is why it's difficult to disconnect completely from social media and face the world without it. However, we can learn how to avoid excessive exposure to individuals on the internet by slowing down and enjoying our lives more.

Setting Boundaries for Social Media Use

Social media is a part of everyday life, but there are moments when it isn't necessary. When you're on social media, whether you have your phone or tablet in hand or placed on the table before you, be mindful of what you're doing and why. There are ways we can be mindful of our daily lives, which would allow us to stop wasting our time on social media. If you're taking a break from social media, then make the following changes:

Sometimes, there are just things we want to do that are irrelevant to our lives, so when we go on social media, it can be tempting to post about them. When you feel like you're indulging in something unnecessary, set a boundary, so you'll know when you're supposed to be on social media and when not.

Set the alarm. If you don't want your phone anywhere near bed at night or while trying to sleep, set the alarm so your phone doesn't try to get your attention as often as it would otherwise. There are ways that you can stop wasting time on social media and enjoy the moments in your life. We all get caught up in what's happening online at some point, but it doesn't do any good to put all our focus on those things. Here are some tips that can help you to avoid excessive exposure to social media:

1. Get Rid of Your Smartphone

If you have a problem with your device, the easiest way to break the habit would be not to have it near or take it away from you. Although this doesn't mean that you have broken free from the addiction, it does remove the trigger for most people who are addicted. If you've found a way to break away from your smartphone, you can move on to the next step.

2. Delete Social Media Apps

If you have decided to remove all the apps on your phone, it's time to do so. It would be best if you did this for many reasons, and it's easier than ever. Nowadays, most smartphones allow you to download and remove specific social media apps later. If certain social media platforms need their app, then there is a way for you to take them off your device too.

3. Limit Access to Your Social Media

Some users don't need this option because they found that there are ways to avoid excessive social media exposure. If you've found a way to limit your access, you can be sure you're taking steps in the right direction. There are a few apps available for your smartphone that can give you the ability to limit your access and gain some more control over your life.

4. Consider Regular Exercises

If you're interested in limiting your time on social media and focusing more on physical activity rather than digital, consider exercising at least several times a week. If you work out, it's tough for others to influence or get inside your head through social media. Not only will it help you to slow down and get rid of your smartphone, but it can also help you to stay mentally healthy.

5. Spend Some Time in Nature

Being outdoors is an excellent way to become more connected with yourself and the people around you. If there is no social media accessible, then you have no choice but to enjoy the time you have in nature. Consider spending as much time as possible during your free time, especially if you're looking for a way to break from excessive exposure online.

6. Play Video Games

If you have children or teenagers in your home, they probably don't want to spend too much time on social media. Consider finding video games with them if you're looking for a way to get some of the same benefits from physical activity. Not only will this be a great way to spend some family time, but it can also offer social benefits.

7. Spend Time in Your Kitchen

Cooking is one of the best ways to avoid excessive exposure to social media and focus more on being present in your life instead. This is an excellent way to improve your quality of life and diet if you want healthier options. You can reduce the risk of heart disease and your chances of getting cancer from a life spent online.

8. Check-In with Others

You don't need to be online to check groups and other forms of social media. Stop wasting time there by using this method instead. You can even schedule a date for the next day or week to talk without a screen between you.

9. Talk with Other Real People Face-to-Face

To avoid excessive exposure to social media on your phone, you should consider talking with others in person more often. Even if you're talking about things happening online, it's much better to do so in person, as it can help you feel more connected with the world around you rather than like you're spending time in your bubble.

10. Talk to Yourself More Often

Spending time with yourself out loud can be beneficial, especially if you have been spending a lot of time staring at a screen. If you need some guidance or even just some motivation, then talking to yourself is a great way for you to calm down and keep control over your thoughts at all times.

11. Do Something Creative

Spending time on social media can take away from your ability to be creative, so it's useful for you to find a way to get your creativity back. You can write a song or poem if you're looking for something that doesn't take too much time, or you can spend more time creating art if you want to spend less time on social media.

12. Meditate with an App

If you find it difficult to break free from excessive exposure online, try meditating with an app as soon as possible. Not only will this help you avoid excessive exposure online, but it can also allow you to eliminate some of your stress.

These are just some of the best ways to avoid excessive time online if you are having a problem with social media. Right now, the best thing you can do is to take action and stick with your plan over time. Once you've taken steps in the right direction, it will become easier to break free from any addiction that might tightly hold you. Don't be scared to take the first step, especially if you don't want to continue down this path any longer.

Finding Alternatives to Social Media

If you are ready to get out of the social media world without giving up the benefits of online platforms, then you should consider finding alternatives. Not only will this allow you to take a break from social media without leaving your home, but it can also be a lot of fun. Every day we see an explosion of new social media platforms that claim to be the next big thing. The truth is that none of them can replace the positives of face-to-face communication, and they use more of your time than they should. Here are some alternatives to using social media that can give you the benefits of staying connected without losing track of what you need to get done.

1. *Read a book you've always wanted to read* - Some books like this require focusing ability, but they should help you get through them much faster than most other forms of media.

2. *Play with your pets* - You can find some great games online that allow you to play with your pet. You can also spend a lot of time watching them play on their own or even try to mimic their actions when interacting with each other through social media channels.

3. *Write something* - This can be an excellent way to do something creative and enjoy it as entertainment while you spend time away from social media platforms.

4. *Email someone* - Emailing is still one of the best ways to communicate quickly and easily, so you should use this method often.

5. *Travel* - This can be a great way to enjoy the outdoors and get fresh air. Suppose you're looking for an alternative that combines social media with travel and other fun activities. In that case, you should consider checking out some of the various apps you can use.

6. *Confine yourself to your home* - If your favorite hobby happens to be taking selfies in front of landmarks around the city, then consider making it a priority for you to live at home for a while and avoid these activities in public areas.

7. *Write a recipe* - Not only will this be a good way for you to enjoy cooking as a hobby, but it can also help you to reach new goals when it comes to cooking. You'll be able to check off recipes that you've made and think about new recipes that might become favorites for your family members and friends.

8. *Take photos around your home* - This is a great way to take photos of your favorite parts of the house without trying to get there. The best part is that your home will always look great in these photos, and you'll have plenty of time with them, so they don't need extra editing.

9. *Do that thing you've always wanted to do* - If you've always been interested in gardening, then ask yourself how this hobby might come more naturally to you now that you are no longer exposed to social media.

10. *Write a list of what you're thankful for* - Take the time to think about what's good in your life. This is another excellent way to enjoy a break from social media without noticing it immediately. You'll be able to take a break, but this will also keep your head clear and free of thoughts that could use a break.

11. Go out of town - If you take a break from social media, you might as well find time to go on a trip. You'll have the chance to enjoy your favorite hobbies while taking a break from social media.

12. Start playing games with your friends - This is still a great way to interact with your friends if you don't mind spending time away from social media, though it can take up some of the spare time you expect.

13. Start an online blog - You can still create a blog that you can share with your friends and family, but you'll be able to spend much more time on other activities, such as learning new skills, going out more often, and finding something that you do well.

You don't want to go too far in these alternatives, but they should all be considered part of your social media break. It would help if you even considered finding a way to link some of these activities together so that you don't feel bored or like it's taking up too much time.

Not everyone will find this same solution useful. Still, it should be considered one of the best alternatives for anyone who wants to escape social media for some time without abandoning their interests entirely. Consider why you want to take a break from social media, and then consider how each of the alternatives presented above can help you get more out of your break while keeping you entertained.

CHAPTER 6

Redefining Success

Social Media's Impact on our Definition of Success and the Problem of Comparison

There have been many different ideas as to what success is throughout the history of our world. Some people believe it's all about being happy, while others think it's all about being popular within social circles with lots of money. Before social media came, success was a much clearer thing. Most would-be rock stars had to practice their instruments for years, photographers would spend hours in front of their cameras to get a good shot, and writers would have to finish an idea before it could take shape on the screen. Before social media, businesspeople had to invest time and resources to create something they could sell.

Social media has changed all this, and although it might seem like we are more successful by what we put online, that is not entirely the truth. The truth is that just putting up something online doesn't mean you are successful. It especially doesn't mean you are successful if you don't put any effort into creating it. It is said that the best things in life are worth waiting for. The truth of that statement has never been so clear until now. We are so used to having everything right away that we tend to give up on the whole thing when we don't get what we want. We have failed to realize that it is probably not good for you if something good comes easily. What's more, what happens when our dreams are easily achieved?

We get bored and stop dreaming. Well-being and happiness don't come from material goods or social media likes but rather from self-realization and self-awareness. After all, you cannot know yourself or be happy if you are unaware of what makes you who you are. You must understand yourself and accept it before letting the outside world have a say in your self-worth.

The only way to truly understand what makes you good is by experiencing life yourself. You can do this by taking part in real-life challenges. You can force yourself to learn something new daily, practice talking to strangers, eat new foods and read difficult books. After months of these challenges, though, I sincerely believe that it's not what we accomplish but how we approach them and how we take action, in general, that defines us as successful people.

We live in a society that constantly pushes the idea of success toward material wealth. It's like "hard work" is an excuse to own as much as possible. When you see someone living this kind of lifestyle, then it becomes normalized in your life. What has happened, though, is that social media has shifted our definition of success to something more like popularity. We are now looking at those with thousands of friends on Facebook and followers on Twitter as the pinnacle of success.

These platforms encourage us to present our lives in the best light possible, so we don't look like we're failing. Because of this, we are doing more than just comparing ourselves to those who already have their lives together. Now we're also comparing who has a "better" life than us. Social media has created a situation where it's impossible for us not to compare our lives, regardless of what they look like on the surface.

This shift in what we consider success is not helping us at all, especially when social media have taken so much time away from our lives and pushed us further down this path compared to others. It's not easy to leave these comparisons completely, but it can be done if you want it enough and take the right steps. Social media doesn't just impact how we think about our own lives but also how we think about others. It can be incredibly easy for us to get lost in these comparisons and look at others as much more successful than we are, especially if we don't understand who they are. This is what happens so often with influencers and celebrities on social media. They'll only show this one small part of their life without ever mentioning the difficulties that they've had behind the scenes.

Social media have been shifting us from our path of success and working on a worldly level. If you're looking for a way to redefine success, you should start by getting away from the idea that it's about materialism. Once you learn how to do this, you can use social media more effectively without hurting your self-worth. Before proceeding with the tips in this chapter, it is essential to find out exactly what social media have been doing to define success in the first place. For that, we need to learn a bit about defining success in the first place. Consider that it's been shown that people do operate on a social level. They use the idea of success or failure as the means to their own individual goals, but they also see this as how they judge other people striving for different things than themselves. As such, you should be able to relate this to how you look at other successful people on social media. People usually define success along a materialistic line because it focuses on how much money and how many friends you have as your primary focus. When looking at someone else, we only look at those external items of success, not their true meaning.

As mentioned earlier, social media have been shifting our idea of what it means to be successful. We were never meant to live this way, as that is not how a successful person or family should live. We are meant to do what we do best and let others help us if they want to join us in doing the same things we enjoy. You can begin getting back on your path to success by finding new ways of helping yourself out when it comes to being successful without using social media for help. There are many ways to do this, but we'll focus on the more important items you can work on.

First, you should learn how to accept your sense of self-worth. You need to be able to say that you are worthy of positive attention from others. You don't have to think you're better than anyone else, and you can still want more for yourself without putting down other people who want the same thing but aren't at the same level.

Next, you must realize that you need a support system behind your goals. When you want to start a business, you need a group of people to support you in this venture. When you want to go and get your first job, you'll need people to help you with the job search.

You don't have to be alone in these matters; we must realize this when looking at our friends and family. We can help ourselves by freeing up our time so that we have more of it to focus on other activities that we enjoy doing.

Finally, you must look at your life and find better ways to connect with people. You're not going to be able to do this through social media. By freeing yourself of the idea that social media is a way to build connections, you can redefine success while avoiding some of the problems you've read about throughout this book.

Tips on How to Set Realistic Goals and Value One's Definition of Success

Next, you'll want to look at some of the different ways you can change your life without needing to rely on social media or the lives of others through social media. You should set goals for yourself and then work towards achieving them. When setting goals, you must remember how much time each goal will require. It may not be worth it if it is too long for the long term. Additionally, it would help to consider whether this goal is something you truly want or someone else has told you that you should want. As you work towards your goals, you need to make sure they're real and know what it means to be successful in your own way.

As soon as you begin thinking about success, it's also important for you to start building a support system around yourself. There are many ways of doing this but finding the right people who can help you with your goals is something that will help on the way to success. When we surround ourselves with negative people who bring us down and don't want to see us succeed, we can't set the right goals or move forward in the right direction.

We can free up time for ourselves by cutting back on social media. Social media take up much time and energy, which you must avoid to succeed in the long run. When using social media, we can't accomplish other things we'd rather do – especially when spending time with the people who matter most to us.

We need to look at our lives and figure out what our first steps toward success should be. There is no one way of doing this, but certain things that have worked for others may also work for you. Fortunately, there are many ways through which we can rethink success while getting away from social media simultaneously.

Next, you should be able to lay out your introvert's path to success while still making it work. There are many ways that the path to success can work for you, depending on the number of goals you have in your life and what it will take to achieve them. You may need outside help or hard work to complete everything. You'll have to find out what will work best for you. You can do this by finding motivation by personalizing your goals and starting small to ensure they truly mean something. You can start by finding out where you want to be in a year, and then you can work towards that goal while figuring out how to reach it.

The next step is to think about what will make you happy. Once you know this, it will be easy to start thinking about and working toward your goals. Setting your goals and dreams will also depend on how much time it takes for each goal to get done. If each one takes a lot of time, this may not be worth it in the long run. We must determine the benefits of following through with these goals, which takes time.

Next, you'll want to ensure that you start with the right mindset before anything else, which means you need to know what you already know and your strengths. It's also important for you to look at how other people have achieved their goals by finding the motivation within themselves while not following the path that has been beaten into the ground for others to follow. There are many different kinds of success and paths, but we can come up with our way of doing this if we can think of a better way based on personalizing our goals.

We can also find out what we hate about ourselves by looking for some negativity within us. Once we know what we dislike, we can improve those parts of ourselves. As for the support system, this is also important for us regarding our goals and dreams. We need to be able to tell others about these dreams that we have for them to help us out with achieving them. We don't necessarily have to share our whole story with everyone, but we must let the people closest to us know what we're trying to do. By doing this, you'll find that you'll get some support from other people who can lend a hand when needed.

Another thing that you need is the motivation that drives you towards overall success in your life. You'll need to know what makes you happy, and you'll need to figure out how your goals will help you do this. When we don't see the benefits of following through with our goals, other people around us may be unable to help us as much. We need to find out what exactly we're doing wrong if we're not motivated by what we want to do.

Finally, you should follow through with your goals now that they have been set and achieved. When you make a goal, it becomes crucial to work towards achieving those goals to meet expectations. As long as you're working towards your goals and dreams, you'll need to keep doing so to stay motivated in the long run. You'll also need to make sure you can make the most of your life by doing what you enjoy. Sticking with your goals and dreams for a long time will be easy if you enjoy something.

When we decide what we truly want, we will also simultaneously know who we are. Once we do this, we need to know if someone can help us in our life while going through this process. If we know why we want to be successful, it will be easy to set goals and dreams that mean something to us. We need to look at what we want out of life, and if there are ways to achieve these goals, it will help us get out of a rut. Regardless of what happens, you must ensure you're going after your dreams. If you're not doing this, it is time to start thinking about your life and where it's headed.

Alternative Ways to Measure Success

There are many alternative ways to measure success depending on your goals. Sometimes, you may want to look at money or fame to show that you've succeeded. But if you're trying to figure this out, you should look at something else instead. One thing that you may want to look at is other people's opinions of your success. Normally this means you want to get support from the people around you to help you accomplish your goals. Sometimes, though, we don't want support from the people around us. Sometimes we feel like we're working towards something even if no one else believes it. In cases like these, it's important for us to briefly outline what success means to us personally so that we can come up with our definition of success and ways of measuring our success while still being able to work towards it.

When we feel a sense of accomplishment, this is the best way to show others how we've accomplished something. If you do this, you'll be able to see what different kinds of success can look like while measuring your progress individually. We also need to remember that there is no right way or wrong way when coming up with our definition of success for ourselves. We need to develop a definition that works for us if we want it enough, but we shouldn't feel pressured into doing so by anyone else. For example, the best way for someone to measure their success could be through their education, as it is something you can't fake and will serve as proof for others who will see it.

Perhaps the best way for someone to gauge their success would be by looking at their health, as it will carry over with them for the rest of their lives. The best way for someone to measure success will depend on what they want out of life. To measure your success in this, you should devise something that works and means something to you. We can look at other things when measuring our successes, but this is only one object, not the whole thing. The scale will still matter if we want to get in shape, but there is more than just the scale that determines how healthy we are. Most people nowadays measure success through fame and money. You'll need to figure out what you want for money and fame to mean anything to you. You might want to determine how much happiness or contentment you will feel when you achieve a goal or dream. You should also make sure that you can do something better than what other people are doing with their lives.

Once you know what these things are, you need to find ways of reaching them to make sense and be worth it. This means we must ensure that we're working towards something for it to matter and mean something to us. When we know our goals, it's easy to measure success through money and the amount of fame we get. We could even say our happiness is based on how much money or fame we get.

We need to realize that the happiness we get from having success will change from person to person, which means that not everyone will be happy with this success, and we need to choose what we want out of life. There are other ways to see success in your life; if you want to find these things, you'll need to look at your life. If you're looking at money or fame as a way of measuring success, then you'll need to find a new way for these things to make sense in your life. We should also look at the cost of success in our lives. Sometimes, it will be easy to see how much money we need to measure our success through this. We'll need to know how much money is spent to achieve something, and once we do this, we can tell what it is that we have left over at the end of our lives.

It may not be the best way to determine if you're successful, but we need to consider why we want this success.

Other alternative ways of measuring success are:

Feeling like we're making the most out of life will be easy to measure when we look at the bigger picture. Seeing that we're getting a lot out of life will show us that it's important to keep doing what we love.

We're still learning new things about ourselves - some people want to feel like they have learned more about themselves when they look back on their lives. This may be based on where they've been and how they got there. We'll need to know what it is that makes us happy for us to figure this out in terms of our lives.

Getting stronger as a person - many people want to see themselves as more substantial than before. They might be looking at their accomplishments or merely want to feel like they're bettering themselves somehow.

Getting healthier - many people look for a way to be better regarding how they feel and how their bodies work. We'll need to know what's healthy for us, and we'll need to ensure that we're looking after ourselves in the most critical ways.

Getting closer to other people is an important piece of success because we want deeper relationships with other people when we look back on our lives. We'll need to be careful that we're not doing this in a possessive way, and we'll need to know what we want out of life when it comes to this.

Being smarter - many people want to see themselves as more intelligent, which is crucial to consider as part of our life. We'll need to think about what it is that we can do better for us to be able to get closer to other people in the future.

Getting more spending money - many people want to see themselves as having more money than before, possibly because they had relatively little money or because the world has changed.

Understanding the world better - sometimes, people want to feel like they understand the world better, which may be because they want to know more about specific things or because they want to know what it is that motivates other people. This could also come from a need for power or their desire to be respected and admired by others. How we do this will depend on our purpose and how we measure success in this area of our lives.

Making the most out of life - sometimes, it's easy for us to get confused about how much we can get out of life. We might be looking at what we do and not see the connection between why we're doing it, or maybe we need a new way of looking at things.

Finding out what it is that makes us happy - there are many ways of finding out what makes us happy, so this could be something that you decide to learn on your own or through being guided by another person. It will all depend on who you are and the life that you have had before.

Having children - this is something that many people want to measure success through, and this could be because they need excitement in their lives or because they want to leave a legacy for their children's future. It would be best to look into having children independently, as this will be important for you.

Things that make our lives more meaningful - when we know what we want out of our lives, it's easy for us to see how these things are linked to each other. These things are why we want to live, and they're also why we want to be successful in whatever way possible.

We must realize the way we measure success will change from person to person. Some people might only care about money and fame, while others might have a more detailed view of success. Our opinions of success can change based on where we're at in our lives, where we've been, and what we want from our lives.

We may also find it easier to measure success if we can see how far we've gone since the beginning of our journey. Some people might see their accomplishments as a way of measuring success, while others might want to know how much stronger they are than they were before they started this journey. When we look at all these things in our life, we can easily get confused because they're different things that we want out of our lives, and some people will use different ideas of success than others.

We need to remember that we can measure ourselves as successful in many ways, and it'll be up to us to find what is best for us in this respect. We'll need to do this independently and ensure we're using the best way possible based on what we want out of our lives.

CHAPTER 7

Finding Happiness Off-Screen

The Importance of Finding Happiness Outside of Social Media

Happiness is something that many of us want, but it's not always easy to find because there are so many different things that can get in the way. Many of us want to find happiness when we look back on our lives, and that's why we need to be sure that we're looking at happiness in the right way. It's easy to feel unhappy because of where we are or the things happening around us. We may feel like we lack purpose or that there's something wrong with our lives, but it will be up to us to figure out what makes us happy and how we can fit this into our lives.

Social media can be a great way for us to find happiness in the social aspect of our lives because it's easy for us to talk about things happening around us and get feedback from others about what we're doing. We can also keep up with people we care about if we want this.

The reality is that many things that can make us happy will also be found by being with others. We may find making friends, pursuing hobbies, or learning new things around others easier. We can get our happiness away from social media screens, so we don't want to ignore this part of our lives. It may be that social media makes it easier for us to make friends in new places, but it might be something that won't bring us true happiness when we look at our lives as a whole.

Social media can also make us feel like we're less happy instead of happier when we look at our lives, which might be because we're comparing where we are with other people and then feeling unhappy about it. It can become a problem if this happens too often, making us feel miserable because of what other people have or the things they do in their lives. We need to use social media to find ourselves, but we shouldn't rely on it to make ourselves happy.

Social media can also make us feel like we're missing out on opportunities. We might see other people doing great things or having great experiences, and this can cause us to feel depressed or unhappy about our own lives. It is especially true if we have a bad experience or something doesn't go how we want it to. When we measure our happiness through what other people do, this will always be around us and can make us feel like there's something wrong with our lives when there isn't.

The truth is that we shouldn't look for happiness in what other people do. We should look for it in the experiences that we have and use the experience of others to inspire us. We can measure success through what others have learned, but we shouldn't measure it by comparing it. This is because happiness is our journey that depends on where we're going rather than where others are. This journey will always be different for us, so it's important to find out what makes us happy and then put this into our lives as much as possible.

The following are important to find happiness outside of social media:

a. Happiness isn't a skill we can easily master, so we shouldn't compare it to others. We must look at it on our own and look within ourselves to see what makes us happy.

b. We have different ways of becoming happier, and looking at social media will never make us happier in this respect. This is especially true because it's so easy for us to compare our lives with the lives of others and get confused.

c. Happiness doesn't depend on what other people do or what they do for them, so these things will never make us feel like we're missing out on anything.

d. We have a lot of happiness in our lives even if we don't think we do, so it will be important that we find ways to use what social media has to offer and put it into our own lives.

e. Happiness can be found through looking at our own experiences, so social media will help us learn from others' experiences but won't give us the answers we need.

f. Social media can be very addictive, making us feel like someone else does things better than we do when this isn't the case, which might cause us to feel like something is wrong with our lives if this happens too often.

g. We need to remember that happiness doesn't depend on social media.

Ways to Cultivate Happiness Without Social Media

Social media can be a great place to turn when we want to be happy because so many of us use social media to escape from our everyday lives, which can give us the happiness we need.

However, this isn't always the most effective form of escaping from our everyday lives. Many of us will want to find happiness in other ways and ensure we're not becoming too dependent on social media. Here are some ways that we can cultivate happiness in our own lives without using social media to do it:

- Connect with people through social media, but then take time off when you know you're going to have a lot of conversations with people online, which will give you a chance to think about the things that are going on in your life. It will make you pay more attention to what's important.

- Go out and do things that make you happy, but when you're doing these activities, stop comparing them to what other people are doing. It will help you focus on your happiness rather than compare it to someone else's.

- Find the things that make you happy and then pursue them as much as possible. These will be the things that matter to you and will bring about true happiness for yourself.

- Learn to be mindful of your own experiences, and you can use social media to help you learn from others and see how to make the most of your life. There will be things we can learn from others, but when it comes to our lives, we need to look at what's important for us instead of what someone else does.

- Spend time with family and friends as much as possible because this can help bring about the happiness many crave. We want to feel loved and cared for by everyone around us because this is something that everyone needs from their family and friends to be happy in life.

- Find hobbies that make you happy and use all the technology available to learn more about these hobbies and take extra classes if possible. There are so many ways to find happiness in life, so it can be easy to do things that are important to us without looking at social media.

- Look towards the future instead of worrying about what other people are doing or what we're missing out on because this will usually make us depressed if we do this too often. We need to instead focus on how our lives will be in the future rather than how other people's lives might be going at any given time.

- All these ways can help us cultivate happiness, and we can use what social media offers to make us happy, but it's not always the best way to do this.

We often think that our happiness depends on what other people are doing or where they are in life, so this can make us feel like something is wrong with our own lives if it happens too often. We must remember that our happiness depends on our experiences, so there's no reason we should look at what other people are doing and focus on that instead of spending time with friends or family. This will ensure that we have a much happier life than someone else.

Strategies for Building and Maintaining Strong Relationships

Friends and family are important in our lives, so we must make sure that we spend time with them to be happy. We don't always think about how important this is because we might be too busy, but when it comes to our happiness and the happiness of others, this is going to be an important part of our lives. Here are some ways that we can build and maintain strong relationships with the people around us:

A. Nurture your relationships

- Go out and meet new people. Sometimes it's easy for us to get caught up with our friends or family members, making us feel like these are the only people who matter in our lives. However, this isn't true, and we need to spend time with new people to learn more about them.

- Plan a casual get-together. For example, you can plan dinner or a picnic in your backyard and invite friends and family. This is a great way to get everyone together because it doesn't have to be too formal.

- Go out for dinner or at someone's house occasionally, especially when you're going through hard times with work or with friends/family. When you go out for dinner, ask about other people's lives instead of talking about yours because this can help make your relationships even stronger than they are now.

- Remember to spend time with friends and family members individually. You might want to spend time with everyone together, but this isn't always the best way to learn about each other. It's much better to go out and spend time with your friends and family than to meet them at a party. We need to spend time with each other to have the relationships we want, which will also help us feel more comfortable around each other.

- Listen to your friends/family members when talking about their lives because someone needs to be the one who's in control of their own life instead of everyone else's. When other people ask us how we're doing, we need to remember to focus on ourselves instead of how they're doing because this can quickly become overwhelming for some people.

- Remember everyone's names, especially those you're closest to. This will make them feel special and included in your life, and if you do this often enough, you'll soon have great relationships with everyone.

- Remember to tell people about something wrong in your life. Sometimes we might have negative thoughts or things going on in our lives, but we don't want to tell people because we're afraid they'll think we're wrong. We need to remember that no matter how bad things might be, they're still going to be there regardless of what anyone else thinks.

- Be honest with your friends and family members because you don't want them to find out something negative about you on their own, which they would probably never do if you were honest with them the whole time.

- Remember to spend time with people going through hard times because this could be the only way to realize how important these relationships are.

- When food is served, remember to eat with your friends and family instead of just eating your portion and leaving the table. This can be seen as rude, and everyone will be deprived of food, making them sad.

- Remember to talk to each other when it's easy rather than trying too hard or talking about the same things repeatedly; otherwise, this can get boring quickly.

- Remember to listen carefully because this will help you have meaningful conversations with your friends and family. It will also show them that you care about what they say, which can help build stronger relationships with the people around you.

- When there are pictures taken at a party or something like that, remember to get one of yourself with your family and friends instead of just posting the pictures on Facebook or something like that because this can still be posted on social media, which can make you feel like you're not important enough for other people.

- Ask your friends and family members questions about their lives so that you can learn more about them.

- Remember to touch each other when you're comfortable with it because it will show people that you care about them, and if you do this in a public place, it can be an excellent way for them to feel comfortable around you.

B. Make time for each other

- Set aside time to go out on a date with the person you're most interested in, and make sure that it's not something too formal because this can quickly turn into a situation where your feelings get hurt instead of improving them.

- Make time for each other throughout the week and during special occasions such as birthdays or holidays so you can spend time together when it's important for your relationship.

C. Talk about the past

- Remember what you used to do when you were younger and ask them if they remember them too because this can help you remember things together more easily.

- Ask them more about things that happened in their lives, especially if it was something that you missed out on in your own life that means a lot to them.

- Spend time talking about movies, music, or other things you used to like when you were younger. Talking about the past can help us remember everything together, which can be fun.

D. Talk about your lives today

- Talk to them about your lives today, but don't focus too much on what's going on with work or other obligations. Instead, talk about how you've been feeling recently and why you're feeling good/bad right now. You can also talk to them about how they've been doing in their own lives lately.

E. Think about the future

- Plan out road trips or vacations together and talk about what you want to do in the future, especially if you plan on doing something different from what you've done.

- Talk about your goals for the future and make sure that everyone is involved in these so that they feel like they're a part of things and can be happy for you when you accomplish them.

- Talk about your aspirations for life, and include them when you do this so that they feel like they're a big part of everything. If they're up to it, they can join you in achieving these aspirations because this can be fun for everyone involved.

- Ensure you're not mentioning specific people you don't want to discuss. There's no reason to bring up other people when making plans for the future, and this can make everyone feel like something is wrong with their own lives. If someone wants to be in your life, you should include them in everything you do.

F. Remember who you are

- Set goals for yourself, and everyone else should join with these because it can be fun for everyone involved, especially if they're going after the same things too. If they're not joining, it's completely fine because nobody should feel like something is wrong with them either way.

- Set limits on when you want to do things. Nobody should feel like they can be pushed into doing things they don't want to, which will only make them unhappy.

- Remember what you want to do in adulthood, especially if you're having a hard time at work or with family members. You might not be able to achieve these goals right now, but this doesn't mean it's not all going to work out for the best in the future because it will.

- Remember how much everyone means to you, especially if you need some companionship at any given time, because your friends and family will always be there for you no matter what.

The important thing to remember when building relationships with others is that you shouldn't go into a relationship because of its benefits. It would be best to go into it because you're interested in the person and want to spend more time with them. You never want to be interested in someone for the idea of being in a relationship, but this is something that people often do when they're just looking for something fun or exciting.

We all want a meaningful relationship, so make sure that you take things seriously and build up your emotional connection with each other rather than just having a quick fun time together because everybody always wants to feel good about themselves and have someone else beside them who makes them feel happy and excited about life. As stated earlier, real relationships are the best because they will help you get more support and make more friends to boost your self-esteem and increase your quality of life. If you want a great life, you must learn how to build up these relationships because this will make the difference between having a fun life and a meaningful one.

CHAPTER 8

Building Real Relationships

The Limitations of Virtual Relationships

Virtual relationships are completely fine, and people can have them with each other, but deep down, we all have the same goals in life, and it's not going to help us to build strong relationships when we don't have access to each other. Relationships are one of the most important things in our lives, so it's best to try and make as many positive relationships as possible because this is going to boost your self-esteem big time and make you feel a lot more confident about yourself, which will make you feel a lot better about your life.

Relationships are mostly good for the people involved because this will help them with issues at work, school, or anywhere else. These relationships can also help to prevent each other from having mental health issues, which is truly important for everyone.

Virtual relationships have their place, but they don't have the same purpose as normal relationships because these are usually more of a quick fix than anything else. In a virtual relationship, you can't see the other person in real life, making things much more difficult. You might find some satisfaction with virtual relationships, but these don't last long because people want to share their lives and experiences.

Virtual relationships are completely different from normal relationships in that there's a lot of distance between the two people involved. This isn't the case when you're in a normal relationship, but sometimes we might not be able to see each other for a few days even if we're in the same state. Virtual relationships are still meaningful because they can give you a chance to know someone else more than you would otherwise, but this doesn't have the same benefits as real-life interactions.

Virtual relationships will not help you learn more about each other, save money, be more social, or build up your self-esteem because these things aren't even possible with virtual relationships. This can give you some interesting experiences, but it won't lead to anything great if you want to go down the path of true happiness and fulfilling life.

The limitations of virtual relationships are that they don't involve any real emotion, meaning that you can only feel them to a certain extent.

Research has proven there have been many studies done on virtual relationships and how people interact with others. The findings from these studies show that people tend to interact with others in virtual environments to the same extent as they would with real people, which means that they're not interacting with each other at all.

If you have ever noticed this, you should know that reality is not created by interacting with others who are not there or by interacting with a computer. No computer processes your responses when interacting with other people in real life. Your real-world social interactions will be based on your behavior and those around you.

This means other people can see how you act with them if they do not like it. They could also give negative responses to your behavior, which will cause you to change how you act with them, and if they still don't like it, there could be a verbal confrontation based on everything they've just seen.

The one thing you can be sure of is that you will have real emotions involved in this type of interaction, but this only happens when you're interacting with real people who exist in real life and not virtual characters or images. That is pretty much the limitations of virtual relationships because they aren't really any different from real ones when it comes down to it. All your feelings and emotions are as powerful as they ever were, but the only difference here is that there's no other person to share them with.

The Importance of Building Face-to-Face Connections

Even though most people with access to the internet and social media don't know it, their relationships are severely limited because they don't involve real-life connections. This will make your virtual relationships much less meaningful because you won't be able to enjoy them nearly as much when you know that these relationships aren't connected with anything else in reality. This is why people who live in the same state as someone else will often try and meet up with each other at some point because they want the benefits that this provides, but this will allow their dreams to slip through their fingers once they realize what's going on.

Imagine going on a blind date with someone and discovering they're weird. You probably wouldn't want to hang out with them again. This is what will happen if you don't build up face-to-face connections because most people aren't going to know about your good qualities or bad ones. If you've ever wondered how your personality is going to be viewed by someone, then this might help you to understand how important these types of connections are. It will allow you to interact face-to-face with people that matter, so you should never settle for anything less than this.

The social media revolution has brought us a lot of things that have changed how we live our lives. However, the one thing that it has not changed is the fact that face-to-face connections are still essential in today's world, meaning that if you want your relationships to be fulfilling, then you will want to make sure that there's some real-life connection involved because these types of things can't be replaced.

Virtual relationships are great for getting to know someone, but if you want to make your relationships more meaningful, you will want to find some way of meeting up with them in person. This effort will make you appreciate how important these types of connections are and might even change your mind about the virtual ones that you have now.

Virtual relationships are great for giving everyone a taste of what real-life connections can provide, but they will fall apart quickly if you don't create face-to-face connections with the people involved. If you limit yourself to one type of connection or the other, you won't be able to enjoy your relationships nearly as much as you could if you had both.

You should know that many benefits come with face-to-face connections, which is obvious when someone doesn't have them. If someone has no idea what being in another person's presence is like, they might not be able to recognize the simple things you do for them, which means that they aren't going to appreciate all of your hard work.

The benefits of face-to-face interactions are:

1. You are better at reading people's emotions.
2. You are more likely to cooperate with other people.
3. You feel closer and more connected to your social group members.
4. You learn much from others by reading their body language and facial expressions.
5. You can empathize with others on a deeper level and understand their feelings and emotions a lot better than when you're just interacting with them online or in a text message format because this doesn't allow you to see them or hear them talking in real-time, which means that you'll have to spend more time thinking about what they're

saying instead of paying attention to their body language, facial expressions, voice tone, etc.

The one thing you can be sure of is that virtual relationships offer many benefits, but they will not be nearly as effective as real-life ones if the people involved don't have face-to-face connections. If you want your relationships to last for more than a short period, then you'll want this type of communication in them because there are so many ways in which it can enrich your relationships and make them more meaningful.

When you build face-to-face connections, you'll get many benefits that aren't available in virtual relationships because these things are only found when there's an actual person involved. This will allow you to have the one thing everyone looks for when they plan on getting close to others: a sense of security, a feeling that's hard to find in many other places.

The only way other people will know how big a part of their life face-to-face connections is supposed to be is if they can experience them themselves. If you tell them that any relationships they are involved with will be lacking unless they create real-life connections, this might help them see the importance of face-to-face connections.

If you're looking for a long-lasting relationship, you will want this type of interaction because many things can be gained from these types of connections. There is going to be one thing missing if these types of interactions aren't included, which is an understanding with the other person on how their actions will affect your emotions. Therefore, the best way to get these types of connections is to find the right person and get to know them face-to-face, like in a traditional relationship. If you're not doing this, you need to start making real-world connections because they are much more effective in every area of your life and will help you become a better person. These types of interactions can add so much value to your life, which is why you shouldn't limit yourself regarding the types of relationships you will have.

CHAPTER 9

Building Resilience

The Impact of Social Media on Our Resilience

Resilience is the ability to be flexible, adaptable, and resilient in different situations; today, more than ever, it is important to have strong resilience. It will help if you have strong psychological resilience to survive in today's increasingly competitive digital world with its fast pace. There are several ways you can do this, and building virtual relationships is one of them, which will lead us into this chapter on building your resilience as a person.

One of the best ways to build resilience is through face-to-face interactions and real-life connections with others because the benefits are large. If you have no idea of the impact these types of interactions can have on your ability to be resilient, then you won't be able to experience these benefits, and that's why we'll look at them in great detail.

This is why you need to make sure that you have a very high level of tolerance for coping with stress, and in today's connected world, it is much easier to overload your brain with stress. Suppose you plan on getting involved in the latest social media craze or have recently paid for your business account for one of these social media sites. In that case, you will be constantly bombarded with notifications that will bring stress into your life.

Some of the major impacts of social media on our resilience include the following:

1. It's extremely easy to get involved in social media but not as easy to get away from being connected. Social media sites will make you feel like you're a part of something big and that so many people are having fun on these sites, which is why you want to become a user. Once you've become a part of this community, it's not easy for you to get away from it because notifications will constantly pop up on your screen, reminding you of all the fun things people do. They'll also give you scores or comparisons of how much more popular or well-liked your friends are who use these sites.

2. It is a very common phenomenon for people to become obsessed with social media, which can lead to them becoming depressed. Social media is now the number one source of depression in the 21st century due to these websites causing users to compare themselves with others. Suppose you're planning on using social media sites regularly. In that case, you're going to want to be sure that you're careful about whom you follow and what type of content you read because this will determine just how much joy or depression you'll end up getting from these sites.

3. It's easy to get involved in social media but very hard to avoid.

If you find yourself addicted and need the social support of others, then you're going to be constantly reminded by these sites of your depression levels, which will cause them to rise. If you have a history of depression or mental health issues or struggle with stress, constantly having these messages on your screen can be extremely depressing. This is why you must prevent your mind from gaining access to these sites for most of the day.

4. Stress is caused by addiction, which makes us always want more even when we aren't getting what we want from our addiction (Facebook). It is a dangerous phenomenon that can cause you to become depressed, sleep deprived, and distracted.

5. It's easy for people to fall into a habit of procrastination because they have social media as an alternative way of spending time instead of working, which is why it's so important that you learn how to overcome this habit if you have trouble with it.

6. It's easy to become depressed if you're always comparing yourself to others on social media, and this can cause you to feel bad about yourself.

7. It's very easy for people to do things they don't want to do when they're constantly reminded that everyone is having fun or missing out on everything by not having a smartphone and being a social media addict.

8. You don't need to use social media to keep up with what your friends are doing, but it's easy for these sites' notifications to interrupt your work.

9. It's easy to become a watcher or stalker on social media, which is why you mustn't feed into the current obsession that people have with these websites and instead treat them like any other addiction because, in the end, you will be a loser if you let yourself get involved in this type of activity.

10. It's easy to become addicted to social networking sites. After several months of doing this, it can cause you to turn negative towards your relationship with those closest to you because they may be an individual on one of the sites. They might feel they are losing their friendship, which can cause difficulties between them and you.

11. The inability to function in society due to a lack of control over your emotions and how your brain reacts. These are some very serious impacts that occur when you overload your brain with stress, but there is also an impact that people never thought about because it pertains to our resilience.

12. A deep sense of alienation and loneliness - This feeling isn't necessarily connected to social media, but a lack of connectivity still causes it. If you're having difficulty connecting with others, this will be a stressful experience for you and will cause your mental health issues to worsen.

This is why you must make sure that your brain is being fed with the right amount of dopamine so that it can stay resilient and not become addicted or depressed and, instead, help you to be able to cope with stress both in the moment and the future.

For your brain to become more resilient, then you must make sure that stress is being prevented from entering your system by keeping social media out of your life for most of the day because when this happens, it will take away a good number of the stresses from your life and this is why you must prevent stress from entering your system as much as possible.

Building Resilience in the Digital Age

Most people today cannot build their resilience because they don't know what it is and don't know how to develop it. When you build resilience, you need to stay focused on one thing at a time, and most of us can't do this in today's world, where we're constantly bombarded with notifications for everything we do online.

In today's world, it is hard for people to build their resilience because they're constantly being distracted from one thing to another by the notifications from the different social media sites they are on. This is why they need to build real-life relationships that allow them to create this type of resilience.

The different social media sites are making it harder for everyone to develop their resilience because they're constantly bombarding us with notifications that we have updates. These things are supposed to make our lives easier. In reality, they're not doing that at all.

Most people believe that resilience is an emotion, but it isn't; it's something you do daily instead of something you feel. Resilience is a skill, and you can work on it daily so that you're able to keep yourself focused on one thing at a time. Even though you're not emotionally resilient, chances are that you will feel this way at different times in your life because of all the situations you find yourself in. For example, suppose someone is building their resilience. In that case, they could occasionally be very upset, depressed, or frustrated because they can't control everything in their life, which we all experience occasionally. If you're not emotionally resilient, you will have a hard time with your life because you cannot deal with the emotions you are experiencing in the best way possible.

Emotional resilience is not something that a lot of people today know how to have, so if they're constantly feeling stuck, stressed out, or depressed, then they need to focus on developing their emotional resilience. Emotional resilience will help you deal with life better, so there are no more issues and problems when dealing with different negative emotions that come up from time to time.

Some people believe that resilience is something you're going to feel in your heart, so if you think that you're feeling a lot of emotions in your heart, then it's probably true. Suppose you're feeling a lot of anger. This is another example of emotional resilience because this can help you deal with upsetting things instead of being dependent on the internet or any other outside source for help.

Suppose everyone needs to learn how to build their emotional resilience. In that case, they should be able to stay focused on one thing at a time and not be concerned about other things simultaneously, which allows them to build their resilience.

The best way to develop your level of resilience is by learning how to do it. It is a skill you can learn from others, from what you see on the internet in books, or even from other people you hang out with daily. To become more resilient, you must surround yourself with resilient people who care about your feelings.

You should also be able to eliminate your negative emotions as quickly as possible, so they don't interfere with how everyone else feels. If you want to learn how to build your emotional resilience, you should be able to get rid of all the negative emotions you may have as quickly as possible.

It would help if you learned how to deal with the emotions you are experiencing so that you don't become upset or frustrated instead of building your emotional resilience. You should also be able to control what happens in your life and whom you surround yourself with so that this doesn't affect your emotional stability.

We are becoming less resilient because we're constantly being bombarded by all of these different notifications, which is why it's so important for people in the modern world to build their emotional resilience. To develop emotional resilience, you must practice focusing on one thing at a time daily and not be distracted from important things.

The only way you will be able to build your resilience is to limit your time on social media and focus on building real-life relationships instead. We're becoming less resilient and more addicted to social media; therefore, if you want to build your resilience, you must ensure that you have the proper social media etiquette in this area and everywhere else. Everyone needs to learn how to build resilience because this will help them become better people instead of adding stress and pain to their lives.

Many people are going through life feeling stressed out and frustrated because they're constantly being distracted from one thing to another, so they can't focus on one thing at a time. We're constantly being distracted by the different notifications we receive from these social media sites. People spend too much time on their computers and smartphones, so they're going on these sites, which is why they become addicted to them because the notifications keep coming in fast. Everyone must have the proper social media etiquette, so this doesn't happen. It's not easy building your emotional resilience, but people must try to do so if they can access it. One can use many emotional resilience exercises to create strength, ultimately making them feel a lot better than they currently do.

One of the best ways to build resilience is to realize that every person has an individual personality. Sometimes, we cannot change everything about ourselves, no matter how hard we try. Letting go of the things you cannot change yourself will be the only way to overcome any obstacle in your life and develop your emotional resilience. Many people are becoming more emotionally unhealthy because of all the stress in the world nowadays, which is why it's so important to have the proper social media etiquette to build our resilience.

Besides building your emotional resilience, you can also create your self-esteem, and you will feel better about yourself when you do this. Some people may not know what they're talking about, so do not let anyone else's opinions influence you. Social media makes many mentally unhealthy, so we must build emotional resilience.

Strategies for Overcoming the Negative Effects of Social Media

Social media is something that everyone seems to have an opinion about and or have an idea about. If we are not careful, we can be negatively affected by what is said online. Sometimes, we may even go as far as tailoring our behavior to this negative influence.

There are many negative effects of social media that we can experience, such as becoming addicted to it and even developing a mental illness because of its influences. It is why we need to build our resilience to overcome the negativity around us. It's easy to get caught up in another's life because they post pictures and details of their lives all over social media, which makes us feel like we want to know as much as possible about them so that we can get a better idea of how they live their daily lives. To become healthier, you need to be more optimistic about life because this will help you deal with negative emotions and improve your life. If you cannot change something about yourself, you need to realize that and not let this affect your everyday life.

Sometimes we get overwhelmed by our negative emotions toward ourselves, so it's important to take a step back and realize what is happening. Overanalyzing situations or trying too hard to improve them can make things worse instead of better. The only way to become emotionally healthier is to truly understand how you think and feel so that you start to develop a healthy relationship with yourself. Keep yourself at a healthy weight, eat healthily, be positive, and don't let anything stress you out.

Everyone needs to know they cannot let one person dictate their entire life because someone can either make them happy or depressed. You will become emotionally healthier if you realize this and do not let it affect your everyday life.

When we become addicted to social media, more negative things come in at us, and our mental health suffers.

Some strategies for building up your resilience include:

1. Finding a Purpose in your Life

The more you focus on what is important, the less time you spend on social media. Many scientific studies have been done on the effects of social media, such as Facebook and Twitter, and they have found that when people are too focused on their phones, they are more likely to become socially anxious. Being socially anxious affects many people's lives because we always feel like others are watching us. This can cause us to be uncomfortable, eventually becoming addicted to our phones. This is why we must build emotional resilience to deal with all the issues around us. Finding a purpose in our lives is the only way we can truly be happy.

2. Getting Rid of Negative People

If you want to remove people from your life, you need to do so because if they are not there, you will have more time to focus on building your emotional resilience. The more negative influences around us, the more likely we will become just like them because this causes us to internalize everything that others have said about us, and this will ultimately cause us to become mentally unhealthy. The people around you have a huge effect on your life because it is important for you to build your emotional resilience to become the best person you can be. It is the only way our lives will improve, and we will prevent ourselves from becoming any more negative than we already are.

3. Surrounding Yourself with Positive Influences

There may be a lot of positive influences in your life, such as friends and family, but sometimes it could be more beneficial for you to surround yourself with strangers who don't know anything about you. This will cause you to be more comfortable around strangers than with someone who has known you your whole life because when you are around someone you are familiar with, they may strongly influence your behavior. If anyone in your life may influence how you live, you need to eliminate them immediately because this can prevent you from building emotional resilience. The fewer negative influences we have, the better chance we will become happier and more positive people.

4. Building a Strong Network of Friends

Having a strong network of friends can have a big impact on your life because having this will cause you to become more emotionally stable. Everyone needs to have the proper social media etiquette because not only does it help us to feel less lonely, but it also helps us to feel less depressed as well.

5. Avoid Perfectionism

The more you try to be perfect, the more other people may start to see you as someone with no flaws, which will cause them to feel they can treat you any way they want. We must build emotional resilience to avoid falling apart at others' words. To become healthier, we need to be the best we can be, which is why overcoming any negative influence we may encounter is important.

6. Avoid Being a Victim

The more you think about the things that happen around you, the more likely you are going to feel depressed, and this will harm your life. Thinking about all the negativity in your life will only cause you to become upset, which will negatively impact your overall health because all this negativity will cause you to go into a state of sympathetic arousal that prevents you from healing.

7. Finding Self-Compassion

Even though it's okay to have feelings of self-pity and anger, it is important to be able to find some compassion for who we are and what we've been through because the more that we focus on how bad our life is, the more others will start to see us as a victim which will cause the person holding themselves back from becoming better.

8. Accepting What has Happened

Sometimes things can get really bad when someone judges us for something that happened in the past. It can cause us to feel extremely uncomfortable about ourselves, ultimately making us depressed. The more we accept what has happened, the more we can start to feel less uncomfortable, and this will help us to be able to deal with all the bad events in our lives and not become depressed about them.

9. Avoiding Social Media Addiction

There will always be people around you who will want to spend as much time on social media as possible because they don't have anything better to do with their time. This is why it is so important for you not to fall into the same trap and start spending too much time on social media because it could cause you many problems later in life when you're trying to build your emotional resilience.

10. Becoming Conscious of Your Thoughts

We all have a lot of negative thoughts floating in our heads, which will eventually cause us to become mentally unwell. This is why it is so important for us to go through the things we think about so that we can understand what's going on in our head because it could be causing us mental and emotional distress.

11. Becoming Aware of Our Feelings

There will be a lot of emotions that we experience throughout our lives, and we need to learn how to deal with them effectively so that they don't have any negative consequences on our lives. If we know how to deal with our emotions, it will be easier for us to become healthier and more positive.

12. Beating Emotional Reactivity

Being emotionally reactive happens to many people, so we must learn how to deal with this negative behavior. This will prevent us from building our emotional resilience because we will be continually triggered by many different things that occur throughout our lives which will cause us to become mentally unwell.

13. Stop Being Hard on Yourself

It's okay if you have done something wrong, but it is never okay if you're constantly beating yourself up over your small mistakes. It is a big issue that happens to everyone, but they don't take the time to examine it or deal with it effectively. It would be best to stop giving yourself so much stress by beating yourself up over small mistakes because this will only cause you more damage and make you feel worse about yourself.

14. Avoid Comparing Your Life to Others

There will always be other people around us who are doing better than we are, so we need to learn how to not compare our life to other people's lives which can cause us many problems in the long run when we are trying to build our emotional resilience. It's okay if you have less than someone else, but focusing on this problem while you go through your life is never okay. The less that we focus on the things that other people have, the better chance we will have of becoming positive and happy people.

15. Focusing on Other Things

The more that you focus on the negative things in your life, the more likely it will be for you to become depressed, and this is why it is so crucial for us to be able to live our lives with positivity because if we do this, then we are going to feel a lot better about ourselves and not let anything wrong get in the way of our happiness.

16. Learning to Keep New Friendships

We need to learn how to build and maintain new friendships because this will help us become happier and healthier, ultimately leading to more positive people. It is also a great way to help others through your own experiences because you can be honest with others and share your own stories with them.

17. Accepting What We Can't Control

There will always be things out of our control in life, and we need to let go of these things to focus on the things we can control. We need to be mindful of the things we can control in life because this will make it much easier for us to become positive people and overcome all of the issues we currently face.

So, if you haven't started becoming more aware of your thoughts and feelings, you need to start doing this to live a less stressful and more enjoyable life.

Logging Out

CONCLUSION

The era of social media has become a very powerful and influential part of our current society, so it is important to learn how to use this technology in the most beneficial way possible. Social media can be used for many good purposes, but it can also be used for many bad intentions as well. If you want to create a positive impact on society, you need to learn how to use social media correctly because if you don't, then there's no doubt that this technology will cause many problems throughout your life.

The more we use social media correctly, the more we can help others through our own experiences, and the more life will feel better.

We all want to live the best possible life, so we must learn how to use social media correctly. The truth is that it may have long-term consequences for us as a society, so we should be more cautious of what we say and do on this platform.

This is one of the reasons why we need to use social media positively. The more we use social media positively, the better chance we will have of creating a more positive society. We want to live a life where people care for others and are more compassionate towards one another. This will make it easier for us to create a society where everything is much more peaceful. So, what we need to do is get as many people online as possible and show them how to use social media correctly so that they can help us create a more positive society. We need to stop acting like people are not responsible for their actions because this should not be the case. People will always act out if they have no internal control over themselves.

The truth is that social media will never cause any problems within our society, so we should use this platform for good purposes because it will help us become happier and healthier people in the long run. Thank you again for reading this book, and I encourage you to log out of social media and redefine what success means to you. It would be best if you never became caught up in the hype of online social media because it is becoming much more negative nowadays than it used to be. It would be best to remember that real people would support you and care about what is happening to you.

The truth is that technology will never be able to experience things for us, so we should try our best not to rely on this platform too much, especially when trying to have fun and enjoy ourselves. We need to make it a point to disconnect our devices anytime we are bored and let ourselves enjoy the things around us. For technology to ever be helpful, we must stop allowing it to control us; this has become an enormous problem. I know that you will succeed in redefining what it means to be successful and building a healthy relationship with yourself because the truth is that if you never become happy in your own life, then there's no doubt that you will never have much success in your life.

It is easier for us to succeed in all our other ventures once we become happy with ourselves because we will start to feel more energetic, motivated, and confident. So please use this time to appreciate yourself and focus on your happiness because you deserve it. Thank you for taking the time to read this book. I hope it has been helpful, and I wish you all the success in positively impacting your own life and the lives of others. We need to make sure that we stop looking for perfection within our lives and start looking for improvement instead. There will always be problems in our lives, but we need to accept these problems as a part of who we are and learn how to move forward in life with gratitude. It is okay to make mistakes because mistakes help us learn what not to do next time, so embrace your mistakes, learn from them, and move forward with a more positive attitude toward life.

I hope you have enjoyed this book and learned a lot from it. I'm going to leave you with one last thought. Today is your tomorrow, so make sure you go there grateful for the love and support surrounding you. You are worth much more than you think, so don't be afraid to show the world that. Don't be scared to stand up for what's right and speak out in the name of love because the best thing about you is your courage to do this, so make sure that you don't hold back on this particular part of your personality because it will benefit all of humanity in a big way.

That said, I want you to have fun with technology because, without technology, we would never be able to have this conversation today. We need technology in our lives just as much as we need love, family, friends, and food, so we must respect this platform while we still have time. I wish you the best of luck and thank you for reading this book. I hope that you will continue to improve yourself and remain positive in the future. Be sure to share this book with your friends and family because we can create a much more positive world if we all learn how to use social media correctly. Have fun, enjoy life, and be thoughtful!

Manufactured by Amazon.ca
Bolton, ON